HOW TO NOT WASTE
MONEY ON

CSR

(CORPORATE SOCIAL RESPONSIBILITY)

KIRILL SMOLYAKOV

Published in the United States of America
ISBN 979-8-3269-2918-1

ACKNOWLEDGMENTS

I dedicate this book to my beloved family. Without them, the book could not have appeared. Each of them made a unique contribution to its preparation.

First of all, I thank my lovely wife, Tatiana, for believing in me. She convinced me to sit down at the table and start writing; otherwise, all this would have remained in the form of oral discussions with colleagues and pleasant memories.

I am incredibly grateful to my daughter Kristina, who became the book's first editor, proofreader, and critic.

And, of course, I am proud that my son Vladislav created the cover design for this book and thereby inspired me to speed up the work on it.

Contents

Chapter 3

Chapter 4

Chapter 5

References

PREFACE

Every morning, when I walked into the MIT Sloan School of Management building for lectures, I saw a large inscription in the main lobby: "The mission of the MIT Sloan School of Management is to develop principled, innovative leaders who improve the world." Every day, I had a cup of coffee before classes, looked at the inscription, and thought that somewhere, I have already heard a similar expression... One day, I realized that I have written and said many times about how CSR is aimed at improving the world. By that time, I already had almost 20 years of practical experience in the field of public relations (PR) and corporate social responsibility (CSR), and I had a lot to analyze over the past years.

The other part of the phrase talks about the principled leader. Integrity is a moral and ethical category, a particular quality of a person; this is not the subject of this book. Although there are many examples in history of how large corporations and their managers, declared their commitment to the principles of CSR and occupied the top positions in the ratings of the most socially responsible companies, became involved in corruption scandals, were caught in fraud and distortion of data. In this regard, discussing the integrity of the business structure here is inappropriate. Integrity in business has a tactical meaning, such as the ability to admit mistakes in a timely manner and apologize in order to avoid more severe consequences.

What about innovation? What innovative forms of CSR and new results can we talk about now? Where and what should employees responsible for CSR in business structures learn? Can there be innovations in CSR, and what are they?

Of course, we are not talking about the use of innovative technologies, which are only tools for successful CSR activities. The point is not at all how the population is informed about a business's social activity through Facebook and Instagram or with the help of leaflets and public hearings.

To become innovations, new ideas or technologies must create and increase value for the company; that is, they must be commercialized. Can new CSR approaches and practices be commercially viable, or in other words, make a profit? And if they can, who benefits from them? If a specific company introduces, for example, green technologies and receives additional profit from this, then what is the basis of this activity, profit, or concern for the environment? What comes first?

In essence, any legitimate business activity aimed at obtaining maximum profit is inherently socially responsible, because it creates jobs, generates taxes which in turn support public institutions, and complies with and improves environmental requirements.

In this regard, innovation is only valuable methods, forms, and technologies for implementing new approaches, including in the field of CSR, that reduce costs, at least if they do not bring profit. It would be correct to call various innovations CSR initiatives.

8

However, since the word innovation has long been used about everything, I am not against its free use in relation to CSR. The main thing is that the uncontrollable desire to be innovative does not violate the basic principle of working with society: to identify stereotypes of public consciousness in a specific place where social activity efforts are being applied and use them to create new value, and not try to change stereotypes or fight them by imposing your own ideas about the best on society world.

Emerging in the mid-90s, the concept of CSR sought to redefine the role of business in society. It proposed that corporations should not merely exist to use resources, produce goods, make profits, and pay taxes. Instead, they should take actions that benefit society and the environment. This shift in perspective was a call for businesses to extend their focus beyond profit and contribute to the well-being of society, thereby improving the world.

Unfortunately, many local community leaders began to use this point of view for selfish purposes, inciting communities to protest against business structures by making unreasonable demands on them. At the same time, such communities are not particularly interested in how profitable the business is at the moment.

Every CSR manager solves two tasks for himself every day. On the one hand, the CSR manager is bound by corporate procedures, standards, and policies. CSR activity is an expensive process, and a CSR manager cannot help but take into account how successfully the business is developing and whether there is money to finance programs. In addition, it entirely depends on the current views on the degree of development and depth of social responsibility of the highest-ranking executive of a firm. It is especially essential if the company is small, private, and not a public corporation. The highest-ranking executive is the primary target audience for the CSR manager.

On the other hand, a CSR manager is obligated to interact closely with stakeholders, taking into account their often inflated ideas about the appropriateness and degree of completeness of social responsibility that a business should shoulder.

When preparing a report, a CSR manager will typically present the company's social and environmental good deeds to demonstrate to society and management how high the company's social responsibility is by telling how many schools have been renovated and playgrounds have been built, how waste is disposed of, and how electricity consumption has been reduced as a result of the activities. Sometimes, he even boasts about the amount of money he spent. Usually, the reports talk about the abstract increase in loyalty to the company among employees and the great benefits to corporate reputation. Very rarely in such reports can one see definitions of any real impact of the activities carried out on society and the growth of the company's value. The reason for the lack of figures lies in the imperfection and often lack of ways to measure the profitability of social activities. Company managers do not even set the task of returning money allocated for social projects, which does not prevent them from calling these expenses social investments.

The most unpleasant question for a CSR manager may be: "How would the company's profit change, and what would happen to its reputation if we did not engage in CSR at all?"

The now actively promoted theory of Strategic CSR requires serious attention from business leaders and, at the same time, high qualifications from CSR managers. At the moment, I have not found a higher education institute that would train professionals in the field of CSR at the undergraduate level, except for specific courses within the master's programs in management. However, specialists with a bachelor's degree should be the main workforce of companies implementing CSR programs out in the field. There is nowhere for a person to come and gain knowledge on how to determine, and therefore calculate, the positive or negative social consequences of all company activities using the value chain. It is this knowledge that is necessary to determine the most profitable operations not only in the production and supply of products but also in social activities, to organically link them together in order to help the company focus on attractive areas and, if necessary, get rid of unprofitable business processes.

A pressing question about the advisability of non-market social activities is how this activity can be transformed into market activities aimed at creating value. The determination of the formula for the relationship between CSR expenses and the company's overall financial results is the most significant challenge. The difficulty in determining the degree of influence CSR has on the activities of the company as a whole, is due to the lack of a method for identifying CSR as an independent business process. Another reason is the lack of proper influence of the CSR manager on the development of the company's business strategy. It is difficult for a manager to prove with the help of numbers that interaction with stakeholders will lead to the emergence of competitive advantages for the company, and CSR expenses will become a returnable and, even more so, profitable investment. In addition, CSR is not at the center of the business model of a company's strategic development plan, so its importance and attempts to make an impact are often ignored.

A paradox arises: on the one hand, CSR is a necessary, integral, uncontested element of the business model, and a generally accepted attribute of a modern company. On the other hand, the specific benefit it brings to shareholders needs to be clarified. It's crucial to emphasize that CSR can be a powerful tool for business owners, not just for company employees, local residents, or environmental organizations. Each company is looking for a way out of the paradoxical situation on its own. However, one way out could be the skillful use of several measurable KPIs and a system of quantitative indicators with measurable CSR returns for the business owner.

Due to the massive variety of CSR programs, different scales and business goals, and different stakeholders for the company, for example, online retail and oil services, it is impossible to develop uniform criteria for the effective implementation of CSR projects. Being essentially a voluntary initiative of business, there are no rules formulated by government regulators and no liability for their violation.

Today, there is a wealth of methods for assessing the effectiveness of CSR, each with its own unique benefits and applications. Their list is impressive. Here are just a few of them: Customer Satisfaction Score (CSAT), Customer Retention Rate, Employee Satisfaction Index, Stakeholder Engagement Index (SEI), Net Promoter Score (NPS), Social Return on Investment (SROI), Balanced Scorecard (BSC), and Theory of Change (ToC)), Dow Jones Sustainability Indices (DJSI), Corporate Knights Global 100, Ethisphere World's Most Ethical Companies, Global Reporting Initiative (GRI), the International Organization for Standardization (ISO) 26000, the United Nations Global Compact (UNGC), Innovation Capability Maturity Model (ICMM), Learning Organization Survey (LOS), CSR Innovation Index (CII), KindLink digital platform, Responsible Business Conduct (RBC), Life Cycle Assessment (LCA), Social Impact Assessments (SIA).

Due to the lack of a large number of mid-level management specialists trained in accordance with uniform standards and programs, CSR is often entrusted to employees of the press service or PR, and their task is to create a beautiful picture and not to count on efficiency and long-term effect of the social performance. The impossibility of a professional, reliable assessment of effectiveness leads to the fact that in many companies, CSR activity is used as a reaction to existing external pressure from society or as an element of an action plan to reduce risks.

In most literature on the topic of CSR, it is defined as a mutually beneficial strategy for cooperation between business and society, and CSR programs are a mechanism for implementing this strategy. At the same time, in the social performance report, you will see almost no information about what the company itself received from CSR.

After CSR managers, public relations and communications specialists enter the stage. A PR manager's task is to bridge the gap between social investments and their impact on the company. Therefore, for additional money, they talk about the invaluable benefits the company received from implementing CSR projects. As a result, the costs of carrying out PR activities often exceed the costs of social activities. Messages about the benefits and importance of CSR use different arguments and data. Some are for persuading shareholders and management, others for persuading government officials, and others for society itself.

A significant part of the book describes the preparatory work to identify the needs of society and its expectations of business. This stage makes it possible to determine how to act in a specific historical situation using the methodology of volumetric analysis of stakeholders and not templates outlined schematically. The main innovation in this book is the ability to view stakeholders dialectically in their development and relationship with each other, and not just with the company.

I have often seen how using linear rather than volumetric approaches have worsened public attitudes towards business. That's why I call my methodology for assessing stakeholders a

3D Stakeholder Engagement Mapping and Plan. It is worth noting that the leading role in transforming a 2D description of stakeholders into a 3D model of program execution belongs to the CSR manager and is carried out by him in his daily work when creating and implementing CSR programs. This kind of transformation requires special thinking skills and the ability to understand that stakeholders exist objectively, without a company, and between them, there is a full range of complex relationships.

The only thing they have in common is a non-stop and ever-increasing desire to receive benefits from business, especially if this business is nearby and can be disturbed. In this desire, they sometimes unite against the company, and sometimes they are incredibly jealous of the very fact of interaction between the company and a specific stakeholder, not to mention genuine cooperation. The most important principle of a CSR manager's work is the principle of not harming the company. If you want to sincerely support one of the parties or some group of stakeholders, you may not notice the resulting dissatisfaction with this on the part of the other group. Instead of expecting a positive result, you will have problems on the other side.

I have succeeded in some of the world's most challenging regions and with the most sensitive populations precisely because I did not isolate or categorize them separately. Creating a stakeholder matrix or map is only necessary at the first stage of environmental analysis. However, detail and care when making a stakeholder map are the basis for successful CSR activities. In a subsequent, deeper analysis, it is necessary to identify two vectors. The first vector of interaction is between the stakeholder and the company, and the second is between the stakeholder and the stakeholder. When the relationships between groups within society become clear, all parties divided into groups unite again and appear as a society, but with an understandable inner essence.

From the kaleidoscope of interests of various groups, similar ones are selected, and programs are created along the company-society line. Thanks to this approach, each stakeholder has confidence that CSR programs are designed to meet their specific needs and correspond precisely to their interests. This is the key to the success of a CSR program and efforts to create a better world.

To whom CSR activity should be directed is one side of the coin. The other side is what projects should be to avoid harming the company and how to implement them. The book will not provide a comparative analysis of social projects or list which projects are more effective. In some places, we need to support education; in others, we need to support sports; and in others, we need to support small businesses. There is no difference, and it all depends on the specific companies, location, and financial capabilities. The fundamental importance and success depend on the correct approach to the implementation schedule of a social project.

Stakeholders must clearly understand when the project begins and with what result it ends. This will save the company from being a debtor to the public. What I mean is that projects without a marked end date and without the final result clearly explained at the beginning of implementation can turn into never-ending projects. Endless social projects are the main danger for the company.

As you know, business interests are changeable, market conditions are inconsistent, financial well-being may end, and a streak of losses and damages will begin. The company may want to sell part of the stake in the business project or exit it altogether. The new owner may have his own view on the scope

15

of his CSR activities. It is extremely difficult to explain to stakeholders that the company will no longer do this after several years of supplying drinking water to secondary schools in the area. Everyone has long forgotten about the company's goodwill, which was initially the Water project's basis. The company must and does not fulfill its obligations. Local water suppliers will warmly support this opinion. They will easily organize residents/parents of children to protest and will not forget to involve local authorities to protect against the "arbitrariness" of the company. In a short time, all the good things done over the years will be disavowed, and the company will face serious reputational problems.

At the same time, projects presented as one-time events within the framework of good-neighborly cooperation, supported by appropriate information support, will be striking events reminding about the company's social responsibility and will not become routine societal responsibilities. Such actions can be repeated many times, but it is necessary to clearly indicate the beginning and, most importantly, the end of the social project. Otherwise, it can turn out like in the anecdote: the entrance is one dollar, and the exit is two.

This book is not about one company or project. It does not describe or analyze successful cases in any particular country. The presented chapters collect and summarize the main approaches to the organization, methods of managing CSR activities, and examples of events that can be implemented anywhere and by any company. The book's main goal is to help companies create value and show how to develop CSR projects that would eliminate the negative impact of society and its individual representatives on business development. These ideas result from 20 years of practical, research, and analytical work aimed at effectively using allocated financial resources in creating a system of CSR activity that would ensure the smooth functioning of all company business divisions. This book is about not wasting financial resources to maintain the CSR bubble. It describes targeted activities that can delight the social environment and ensure the smooth functioning of a project or asset. At the same time, it is shown why heavy multi-year strategic programs lead to negative results.

Based on the principles of business ethics, the names of companies, actors, and places where CSR programs are implemented are made up in the book. In fact, the genre of the book is business fiction, and it is composed as a tool chest with dozens of drawers. Any similarities are random. Social projects implemented in different countries are combined, and their results are summarized and presented as one holistic project. The reader may ask, did what is described in the book actually happen? And I will answer: it wasn't like this, but it could have been.

Chapter 1

SURROUNDING
SITUATION

Before embarking on any significant endeavor, a proficient management team must grasp the crux of the matter. This entails identifying the challenges and problematic issues at the forefront. This book delves into the preparation process of the Stakeholder Study and Stakeholder Engagement Plan, highlighting the extensive field, legal, and archive research that the CSR Team must undertake. It's important to note that this is not a depiction of a single company's activities in a specific project but a collective representation of CSR activities based on years of experience. This book, a fictional business narrative, serves to elucidate the CSR methodology in a more tangible form.

The narrative unfolds in the complex and challenging environment of the fictional country Zefuk Republic, where an oil company, RECUSTAT, a product of imagination, is granted the right to develop the massive Upper Banop oil field. Zefuk is riddled with social issues and economic hurdles, setting the stage for a project hinges on the swift and effective peaceful resolution of social unrest.

The arduous task of managing this intricate situation is placed in the capable hands of RECUSTAT'S CSR Team, underscoring the pivotal role they play in this demanding endeavor.

The narrative commences in 2030 and spans the latter half of the 21st century. Over the past century, Zefuk has weathered six wars with external adversaries and one civil war. The country grapples with inadequate education and skill levels, with some regions experiencing an alarming 70 percent unemployment rate.

The CSR team of RECUSTAT must operate in this potentially hostile environment. An additional problem is the imperfection of legislation and its inability to implement it. Some laws affecting the interests of ordinary people were adopted in the middle of the 20th century. They do not correspond to modern realities and international standards. The outdated Zefuk's laws conflict with the principles of compliance with international standards of the 21st century that RECUSTAT follows.

Upper Banop is one of Zefuk's Republic's largest oil fields and is believed to hold 30 billion barrels of recoverable reserves, making it one of the largest oil fields in the world. The field is located in southern Zefuk, 98 miles South of Sadbokan, a major seaport. Most of the project area is agricultural land used for cropping and raising livestock. The area to the West has rainforests with hills and low mountains. The area to the southwest was previously wetland and marshland but has been drained and used for agricultural purposes. Most of the local population lives south of the project area, adjacent to the Bigony River. The Fadosa River runs to the northeast. The area may contain landmines, unexploded ordnance (UXO), and explosive remnants of war (ERW).

The parties of the Upper Banop oil field Development Contract are Zefuk's state-owned Atukaz Oil Company from one side and the Contracting Operator, formed by RECUSTAT Oil Company ("Operator"), from the other side. The agreement will last 25 years with the possibility of a five-year extension. According to preliminary estimates, the Operator's investments in the Upper Banop oil field were expected to reach about USD 500 million in 2030 and USD 6 billion during the following four to five years.

CSR and Upper Banop Development

Corporate Social Responsibility (CSR) is the term used to describe the intention to develop the Upper Banop oil field in a way that makes us a valued part of the local community. RECUSTAT Oil Company invests in the community in which it operates, managing the reputation and operational risks of poor local community relations. RECUSTAT commits to operating the project in accordance with international human rights standards and laws.

The Operator of the Upper Banop oil field, RECUSTAT Oil Company, is deeply committed to the belief that Corporate Social Responsibility (CSR) is not just a choice but a necessity for it to contribute to sustainable development in the countries in which it operates. It actively seeks to foster mutual understanding and a positive relationship with local communities, a pivotal step in bolstering our corporate reputation, ensuring the safety and security of our operations, and obtaining and maintaining the necessary social and regulatory licenses to operate.

In Corporate Social Responsibility documents, the term' stakeholders' is used. This term encompasses anyone who is affected by the project or has the potential to impact it. The key project stakeholders are the state Atukaz Oil Company, local government authorities, tribal leaders, and the local communities in which RECUSTAT operates, who play a vital role in the success and sustainability of the Upper Banop oil field project.

RECUSTAT has to apply international best practices and to take necessary steps to prevent damage of living conditions or quality of life of surrounding communities, and in the event of any-adverse effects, minimize such impacts, and provide adequate compensation for personal injury or property damage resulting from oil extraction.

Corporate social responsibility management is vital to the operation's success and to managing key risks that have the potential to delay or halt operations, particularly in a sensitive security environment. Any delay to the project schedule will have significant financial implications for the Operator and its partners.

The purpose of this chapter is to describe the operational and social risks relevant for the Operator in developing the Upper Banop oil field in the Zefuk Republic. The Joint Management

Committee is responsible for using this document as a guide to reduce these risks. The document addresses specifically the two key risks that are urgent for the project at this stage of its development

- land compensation and resettlement;
- community expectations.

Other social risks to the project that will be considered in the future include:

- Land ownership, relocation, and compensation.
- Community disturbance.
- Vulnerable groups (Indigenous people, minorities, etc.).
- The influx of people / cultural differences.
- Cultural heritage (religious/cultural sites).
- Tribe conflicts/civil unrest.

Local Context

Building mutual understanding and a positive relationship with stakeholders in the Contract Area, the Operator has taken so far, the following measures:

• Establishment of Corporate Social Responsibility Working Group (hereafter 'Social Committee'). This Committee aims to coordinate issues of interaction with local communities in the Contract Area concerning social investment, land compensation and resettlement, local community dialogue, and local content, including local employment and business development.

• Implement grievance and feedback mechanisms between the Operator and local communities through the Social Committee.

• Provision of detailed guidelines and execution plan for land compensation and resettlement of local communities within the area of operations to the state Atukaz Oil Company, which is responsible under the Upper Banop oil field Development Contract for providing the Contract Area to the Operator free of claims by local farmers.

• Implementation of social projects in health, sport, and education.

• Establish a newsletter under the Upper Banop Project to inform the local population about significant project events.

From the outset of the project, the CSR Team of RECUSTAT oil company embarked on a collaborative internal research initiative in Sadbokan province. This research, which involved interviews with 26 local stakeholders, was a joint effort with the Sadbokan Provincial Council, the NGO Coordination Committee in the Zefuk Republic, local Dokemy District and Sub-districts Councils, the Department of Archaeological Inspections in Sadbokan, and the Department of Foreign International Development. This collaborative approach was instrumental in gaining a comprehensive understanding of the local environment. The objectives of the interviews were to understand the attitudes towards investment by foreign companies of local leaders and influential people from the populated areas close to the oil field of Upper Banop.

All interviewees agreed that encouraging foreign companies to establish operations in the Zefuk Republic was positive and necessary for job creation, business growth, infrastructure improvement, and overall local development.

Creating employment opportunities was considered the most essential benefit of foreign companies investing in the Sadbokan province. The development of public services and the transfer of expertise and skills were also viewed as significant benefits of foreign investment.

Most respondents believe that although foreign companies are not responsible for providing public services, they should contribute to local development by investing in infrastructure and community development initiatives.

Land acquisition and compensation were clearly stated as a key risk to foreign companies and a concern for the local community. Indeed, the impact on farmers and the issue of land confiscation were recurrent themes in the interviews.

Security was repeatedly highlighted as a critical challenge for foreign companies, a significant community concern, and a social need. Interviewees especially noted the risk posed by some armed groups involved in violent activities targeting foreign companies.

Most respondents stated that the community would generally welcome foreign companies but would need clear evidence of benefits flowing back to the local population. This highlights the importance to Operator in communicating clearly and openly about their activities and the benefits that their presence may bring to the community.

The survey results demonstrate the importance for foreign companies to communicate effectively with the local community.

Social Risks

Three key risks exist for the Upper Banop at its first development stage. The risks outlined below have been identified by internal risk assessment processes and research conducted in the field by the CSR Team.

Risk # 1 - Land compensation and resettlement

Land compensation and resettlement are not conducted in accordance with international standards. Under the Upper Banop Development Contract, the state Atukaz Oil Company is responsible for providing the Contract Area to the RECUSTAT oil company free of farmer's claims. In this regard, one of the primary concerns of the Operator is the relocation of people living in the South of the project area, adjacent to the Bigony River, to ensure further sustainable development of oil reservoirs. With that, the Zefuki side shall conduct a land compensation and resettlement process in line with international standards. Implementing international standards for the above issue will contribute to the stability of the project's stakeholder environment. The implementation of international standards regarding resettlement will also assist in avoiding stakeholder outrage, which may result in potential delays and reputational impacts that may hinder the project's development schedule.

The Upper Banop contract area is populated, particularly along the Bigony River, which runs west to East through the southern part of the area. Local residents, internally displaced persons, and aboriginal communities also use the area for agricultural purposes, including cropping and raising livestock.

The risk to the project is that compensation and resettlement of persons of the Upper Banop oil field are not conducted according to international standards, resulting in

26

aggression from local communities, which may result in delays to the development schedule, safety, and security issues, and on the reputation of RECUSTAT oil company, and indeed, all international oil companies operating in southern Zefuk.

Given the Operator's standing in the international community, resettlement and compensation must be done according to international standards.

Land compensation and resettlement will be challenging for the Operator and State Atukaz Oil Company to manage. The parties will ensure the appropriate resources are appointed to manage these challenges and that Zefuki laws and international standards are adhered to. This will be guided by a resettlement action plan.

To mitigate this potential risk, the CSR Team will:

• Develop a Resettlement Action Plan (RAP) as international standards require.

• Work with and support the Atukaz State Oil Company, which is responsible under the contract for such activities, to design, forward-plan, and enact a resettlement program to international standards. These necessary measures are vital for the sustainable development of oil formations.

• Work with the State Atukaz Oil Company to begin a dialogue with potentially affected people and the local communities in the area. As the development schedule currently stands, the Operator has until before the beginning of seismic activities to prepare for the land access and compensation requirements of its seismic activities.

• Design and enact through state Atukaz Oil Company relocation and resettlement mechanisms in line with international standards.;

Risk # 2 - Community expectations are not met

To manage these and other social risks, the project will use the approach described in the following areas of corporate social responsibility.

It is noted, however, that other social risks exist for the project and will be considered in the future. They include land ownership, relocation, and compensation; community disturbance; vulnerable groups (indigenous people, native people, nomadic peoples, minorities, etc.); influx of people / cultural differences; cultural heritage (religious/cultural sites); tribe conflicts/civil unrest.

There are two key areas of corporate social responsibility for the Operator for the development of the Upper Banop oil field. The approach to each area is described below:

Social investment

As a good corporate citizen, the Operator will invest in the communities in which it operates in Zefuk through its social investment program. The Operator's philosophy is to support existing initiatives and develop new initiatives by local authorities to improve infrastructure and services in health, education, and basic needs (potable water, electricity, sanitation). There is high expectation from local communities that the project will improve living standards. The risk for the project is that local communities do not feel like they are benefiting from our presence in the area, resulting in conflict. This social investment approach will reduce this risk.

The Stakeholder Study conducted by the CSR Team indicates that the local community prioritizes the following needs for investment by foreign companies:

- Improved public utilities such as electricity, water, health, schools, and roads.

- Infrastructure to develop the local economy, such as rehabilitation of agriculture and improvement of skilled labor (carpentry and iron works, handicrafts).

- Infrastructure to support social life and community interaction, such as sports facilities for the youth and entertainment parks. This category reflects the desire of the community to become a modern society with access to leisure activities and facilities.

Local community dialogue

The Upper Banop oil field area and surrounding regions are highly populated. The Upper Banop project will have both positive and negative impacts on those people. It is critically important to ensure communities feel informed about the project so the CSR Team avoids conflict and potential violence against the Operator's people and assets. The CSR Team is aware that poor local community dialogue has caused conflict and delayed operations of other IOCs in the region.

Local community dialogue is critically important to establishing and maintaining harmonious relations with local communities, which will, in turn, increase the security and overall success of the project. At present, limited local community dialogue has occurred. Because of the project's early stage, local people may not be aware of the Operator's presence. Dialogue must occur swiftly, before the seismic survey, and as an ongoing risk management strategy for the development. The

CSR Team requires the support and involvement of the State Atukaz Oil Company to begin a dialogue to ensure the effective management of expectations in local communities to avoid conflict.

To mitigate this potential risk, the CSR Team will:

• Consult local authorities to align with the existing social development plans (for example, the Sadbokan Governate District Development Plan).

• Develop an annual social investment plan.

• Work with the State Atukaz Oil Company to build trust among the local population and establish a transparent dialogue.

• Develop a Stakeholder Engagement Plan to provide a structured approach that describes the essential key messages about a project, the responsibilities of persons within the project regarding local community dialogue, and the methods that will be used to engage local communities in dialogue.

• Develop and distribute regular information updates to the local community.

• According to the Upper Banop Development Contract, a grievance mechanism will be established to manage community concerns and expectations.

Risk # 3 - Local content (training, employment, local business development)

This part of the corporate social responsibility approach aims to maximize the project's benefit for community members in the Upper Banop area.

Unemployment in the Sadbokan Province is 70%. Creating employment is one of the primary development needs, as it is the most important prospective benefit of foreign investment but also a key challenge for oil companies. The Stakeholder Study mentioned that failing to address this issue or not using the local workforce and local companies is a significant potential reason for opposition.

Investment in human capital (building local workforce capacity through training, transfer of foreign skills, and modern technologies) will be required to raise the industry to international standards. The Operator should explain what opportunities will be available for local businesses to supply goods and services to the project and what types of skilled workers they will need. Furthermore, the Operator should demonstrate a commitment to equipping businesses and workers to the required level.

This will help address concerns about the potential loss of jobs in the agriculture industry and negative impacts on local businesses.

To mitigate this risk, the CSR Team will:

• Create a local employment plan, giving priority to local communities.

• Develop employee training programs (including basic literacy, numeracy, and vocational training).

• Develop a community development and training center (to train in HSE competence and reduce the project's safety risk).

• Support the development of local small businesses to provide goods and services to the project.

Conclusion

Forming a Corporate Social Responsibility Committee is necessary to manage the implementation of the above approaches to risk management. The Corporate Social Responsibility Committee will be responsible for updating the strategy and developing a yearly plan based on the strategic direction set by RECUSTAT Oil Company corporate standards.

The Corporate Social Responsibility Committee will comprise representatives of:

• Atukaz State Oil Company

• RECUSTAT Oil Company

Membership will include persons with Corporate Social Responsibility, HSE, Security, human resources, and legal expertise. Establishing the Corporate Social Responsibility Committee will be a resolution for consideration by the Joint Management Committee.

Later in the book, I will explain how the decision to create the Social Committee plays a vital role in ensuring smooth oil operations and avoiding mass protests and work stoppages.

Chapter 2

STAKEHOLDER STUDY

Approach to developing stakeholders mapping

RECUSTAT Oil Company instructed the CSR Team to conduct a stakeholder study for the contract area of Upper Banop oil field (referred to in the book as Upper Banop) while preserving the anonymity of RECUSTAT.

The field of Upper Banop is located around 98 miles South of the capital city of Sadbokan in the Sadbokan Province. The size of the Upper Banop contract area is 49 X 35 miles and is delimited to the North by the Northern Province, to the South by the populated District of Dokemy located on the Bigony River, to the West by the Western Province, and the Rainforests and Marsh Areas and to the East by the North-South Canal (which was completed in 1991) and is commonly referred to as the "River," 8 miles West of its confluence with the Fadosa river at the Village of Riverland.

Timeframe

The CSR team received the task and agreed to a 12-week study and evaluation program for the Upper Banop project, which began with a workshop in May 2030. The draft report was submitted in August 2030.

Limitations

Fieldwork was conducted over six weeks during June and July 2030. Summer heat and the difficulties associated with electricity shortages may have skewed responses regarding investment and development priorities.

Although the CSR Team managed to meet and interview women and women's representatives, most of the stakeholders interviewed were men. The rural and urban communities living in this area are patriarchal and access to women can be difficult. As per RECUSTAT's request, all field research was conducted under the name of the CSR Team to preserve its anonymity. The CSR Team also did not disclose to interviewees that the research was for the oil and gas sector. The findings must be considered in this context. RECUSTAT should be careful not to rely solely on this research for stakeholder engagement and social investment plans, which will be developed in the coming months.

Team

The CSR Team, in a collaborative effort, mobilized a field team of 5 consultants to undertake the fieldwork. Two employees managed the project in the CSR Team's office, while others provided their expertise and inputs on the engagement strategy, planning, and resettlement guidelines.

The locals, playing a crucial role, have gathered field data and interviews in their native language. This data was then assessed in the office to preserve meaning and ensure that no information is lost in translation.

Methodology

Research and data gathering was undertaken through:

1. Interviews with key stakeholders on-site at the District and Sub-district levels, including government officials, community leaders, and representatives from local businesses, were a crucial part of our methodology. The CSR Team's local data collection staff conducted attitude interviews with these stakeholders using a structured survey. The invaluable insights gained from these interviews form the bedrock of their recommendations on how RECUSTAT can collaborate with stakeholders and Zefuki Republic's decision-making and influence structures.

2. The desk research conducted by the CSR Team personnel in Sadbokan was not just a casual consultation, but a comprehensive exploration. They engaged extensively with contacts in Capital City and Sadbokan, including those working for the Government of Zefuk and donors. Through these contacts and other thorough research, the CSR Team accessed a wealth of resources and documents prepared over the last five years by various agencies.

3. Final research was comprehensive, involving interviews with a total of 79 local stakeholders, ensuring a broad and diverse range of perspectives were considered.

About the location history

The Area of Upper Banop, a region characterized by its diverse natural environment, was once covered by the Rainforests and Marshes known as the Rainforests and Marshes of the River or the Western Rainforests and Marshlands. These lush Rainforests and expansive Marshes, spanning about 2000 square miles, were a unique feature of the area, beginning South of Second City and ending in the Bigony River at Third Village. These Rainforests and Marshes covered about 2000 square miles, beginning South of Second City and ending in the Bigony River at Third Village.

The Rainforests and Marshlands, once a thriving ecosystem in the lower part of the Fadosa-Bigony basin, were severely impacted in the late 1990s. Upstream dam construction and diminishing water flows took a toll on these natural wonders. The situation worsened with the construction of extensive drainage works between 1990 and 1998, hastening the eradication of the Rainforests and Marshlands. These lush landscapes, which in the early 1960s spanned over 20,000 square miles of Zefuk, transformed into a desert landscape and salt flats by 2000, with over 90% of the Marshland area drying out.

Western Rainforests and Marshlands

The 40-mile West-East canal located along the northern boundary of the main Western Rainforests and Marshlands, together with the larger North-South canal, the "River," completed in 1989, effectively drained and prevented the refill of the Western Rainforests and Marshlands. The 'River' is a significant part of the drainage system, discharging the water to the Bigony River at the Third Village, thereby contributing to the transformation of the landscape.

The Dokemy District is crossed from West to East by the Bigony River. Most of the population is settled along its banks. The eastern part of the district is also crossed by the "River." The total area of the district is 1,037 square miles.

The southern part of the district is intersected by the Sweet Canal, a testament to human ingenuity and resilience. This water management system, built in the 1990s, was specifically designed to supply Dokemy District with less salty water, ensuring a sustainable and reliable water source for the community.

The following information is mainly drawn from the Dokemy District Provincial Development Strategy (2007-2009), the latest Provincial Development Strategy for Sadbokan (2008-2010), the New Master report, and CSR Team field research.

Population

The total population of Dokemy District, a crucial factor for decision-making, is estimated to be between 250,000 and 290,000 people, equivalent to 7% of the entire Province. According to a census from the Ministry of Trade, the population of Dokemy District reached 250,000 people in 2027. The total population of the Sadbokan province increases annually at a rate of 3 to 4%. This rapid population growth poses challenges for the district's infrastructure, services, and natural resources, necessitating careful planning and management.

The District has a total of 38 villages and towns. There are 22 main settlements by Sub-districts. The main population centers of the District are Dokemy City, Baka, Third Village, Salo, and Kloss, which all have populations of over 15,000 people. It's important to note that only 30% of the settlements have a population of over 5,000 inhabitants, while the majority have a population between 80 and 5,000. This diverse distribution of population, apart from Dokemy City, reflects the unique character of the District.

All of the significantly populated areas are strategically located close to the Upper Banop oil field's operations. This proximity ensures efficient access to resources and services. The urban areas constitute 33% of the District, while the rural areas equal 67%. While not part of the CSR Team consultation area, recent stakeholder research undertaken by the CSR Team indicates that the local community feels strongly about the important role they may have in the development of Upper Banop. The research findings highlight the potential for opposition groups to emerge from the North, as indicated by respondents in Dokemy. These findings are significant for RECUSTAT and understanding them can help in devising effective strategies for stakeholder engagement.

Population Indicators

Population Indicators: according to the statistics in the Sadbokan Development Strategy, around 52.8 % of the total population of Sadbokan's Province is between 15 and 64 years old, corresponding to the population in working age. In Sadbokan, 49.73% of the population are women versus 50.27% of men. The percentage of the population below 14 years old is higher than that of the same population at a national level (39%). These indicators suggest a potential for a young and dynamic workforce in the District, which can be leveraged for its development. According to the Dokemy Municipal Council, the average family in the District comprises five members, indicating a potential for a large consumer base.

Administration

The District of Dokemy is divided into the three following sub-districts:

- Dokemy (Centre)

- Dokem-1

- Third Village

Dokemy District Local Council is the highest authority over which the mayor and sub-district heads preside.

Skills and Education

More than 80 schools in the District of Dokemy are spread between the 3 Sub-districts. Primary schools account for 70% of the educational institutions operating in the District. 75% of students attend primary school compared to only 17% for secondary school. These figures confirm our field findings that most people in the District have a low level of education. The Rainforest and Marsh people are particularly disadvantaged in education due to the absence or inaccessibility of schools in the Rainforests and Marsh areas and in remote locations and the inability to afford school fees. Because of tribal traditions and local customs, the enrolment of girls versus boys is lower in every grade, particularly in secondary school.

Youth unemployment is very high due to limited job opportunities and a need for more appropriate skills and educational qualifications amongst young people.

Standards of living

In the District of Dokemy, around 10% of men are estimated to be unemployed, compared to over 40% of women. The average income per month in the District is between 85 USD – 255 USD. Most income is derived from employment in the public sector (administration, public services, and security). Agricultural activity is dominant in the area.

However, many of those involved in this sector now live below the poverty line (US$2 per day) due to the decline of the agricultural industry. Many Rainforests and Marsh people have moved to the urban areas seeking public sector jobs.

According to the United Nations Office for the Coordination of Humanitarian Affairs, around 30% of the population, or 68,000 people, lives in absolute poverty in the District of Dokemy.

Housing

According to 2006-2007 data, 42,643 families live in 25,259 houses. This data confirms the CSR Team's findings that two families usually share one house.

Housing is distributed as follows:

• Dokemy Sub-district: 17,544 families occupy 8,504 houses.

• Dokem-1 Sub-district:13,323 families occupy 7,302 houses.

• Third Village Sub-district: 11,776 families occupy 9,453 houses.

Most of the houses in the urban areas are built of bricks and cement; however, in the villages, most houses are made of reeds and mud and are distributed as follows:

• 11% built of concrete material

• 4% built of bricks

• 33% built of blocks

40

- 9% built of mud

- 7% built of reeds

The majority of these houses are old, and the construction material is sourced locally.

Roads and infrastructure

According to the Provincial Council, there are 10 miles of streets in the District of Dokemy, of which only 3 miles are paved. There are 100 miles of roads between the Dokemy Sub-District and the neighboring villages of the Sub-district.

Agriculture

The District of Dokemy represents the Southern regions of the Rainforests and Marshlands. The drained Marshlands have been developed as farmlands. The fertile area composed of arable lands is particularly suitable for growing crops, which is the main source of income for the District, together with livestock and fishing. Agricultural activities predominate in 70% of the urban settlements. These urban settlements include 80% of the total population of the District.

In the 1970s, Dokemy specialized in growing tomatoes in cultivated Marshes. However, this farming declined due to oil exploration and the drying of agricultural lands, rainforests, and Marshes.

Presently, the Dokemy Sub-district boasts approximately 69,000 palm trees, a significant source of dates. The main crops in Dokemy today are barley and wheat, cultivated across a total area of 17,000 acres, out of a potential cultivation area of 42,000 acres.

Cultivated Winter crops	Palm trees	2 700 acres
	Wheat	9 000 acres
	Barley	1 200 acres
	Others	1 500 acres
Cultivated Summer crops	Maize	1 000 acres

Raising livestock is also an important agricultural activity in Dokemy. Key livestock are cattle, buffaloes, goats, sheep, and chickens. According to the most recent Dokemy District profile statistics, 2,519 farmers raise 7,959 buffaloes and 13,677 cows.

Industrial activity

Other than agriculture, the primary industries in the District are ironwork (for steel windows and doors), carpentry (domestic furniture), and cement (producing tiles, blocks, and slabs). According to our interviews, there are 375 factories registered for the Third Village Sub-district, divided into 150 carpentry, 125 ironworks, and 100 construction companies. Third Village is also well known for building fishing boats, which the Rainforests and Marsh people use. The following graph shows the importance and percentage of nine different activities for the three Sub-districts of Dokemy.

Religion and tribes

The predominant religions in Dokemy are Christianity and Islam.

There are 20 tribes in the District. The biggest tribe is Beta, headed by Chieftain Pedro; the Dara tribe is headed by Sheikh Iba; the Budan tribe is headed by Leader Hura; the Sinori tribe is headed by Sheikh Hama; the Hika tribe is headed by Sheikh Anas; and the Subo tribe is headed by Chieftain Mogy.

2029 Provincial Elections

The following are the final election results for Sadbokan Province, announced in February 2029, and the comparison with the previous political period in 2025.

Table 1

Coalition 2029/2030	Seats (2029)	Change	Votes
State Party	20	+17	239,007
New Party	5	-15	74,879
Party of Freedom	2	+2	34,862
Main Party	2	-	32,020
Zefuk Party	2	+2	24,817
National Party	2	-2	21,091
Best Party	1	-11	20,932
United Party	1	+1	227

President's State Party won the most seats in the elections in Sadbokan and in all ten provinces from the South. The results suggest that the voters distanced themselves from the New Party, led now by Jaus Axyneda and closely linked to Ekulon Republic. Indeed, the New Party lost 15 seats compared to the 2025 elections. The results may also suggest growing unhappiness with the religious parties and their ability to govern effectively.

OUTPUT # 1

STAKEHOLDERS MAPPING - WHO'S WHO IN TARGETED REGIONS

The following table was compiled based on the CSR Team's knowledge of the region and information gathered through the interviews. The comments about individuals are subjective, although the CSR Team believes they are based on sound reasoning. Given the sensitive nature of these comments, this table must have minimal circulation within RECUSTAT Oil Company.

Table 2

Title	Organization	Importance in relation to influencing the success	Key decision maker	They influence the opinion of...
Director of Exploration Department	ATUKAZ OIL COMPANY	strong	yes	Board Chairman
Director of Drilling Department	ATUKAZ OIL COMPANY	strong	yes	
Director of Planning	ATUKAZ OIL COMPANY	strong	yes	Board Chairman
Director of Administration	ATUKAZ OIL COMPANY	weak	no	

Director of Water resources Department	ATUKAZ OIL COMPANY	strong		
Director of Engineering Department	ATUKAZ OIL COMPANY	weak		
Employee	ATUKAZ OIL COMPANY	weak	no	Other ATUKAZ OIL COMPANY employees
Director of Station 3	ATUKAZ OIL COMPANY	strong	yes	Other ATUKAZ OIL COMPANY employees
Member of the Provincial Council	Sadbokan Provincial Council	strong	yes	Other members of the council
Member of the Provincial Council	Sadbokan Provincial council	strong	yes	Other members of the council
Member of Municipality Council	Third Village Local Council	strong	yes	Dara tribe and residents at Third Village Sub district
Member of Municipality Council	Dokemy Local Council	strong	yes	Other members of the council
Chairman of Third Village local Council	Third Village Local Council	strong	yes	Residents of his Sub-district
Chairman	Local Council in Dokemy Sub-district	strong	yes	Residents of his Sub-district
Mayor of Dokemy	Ministry of Municipality and Public Works	very strong	yes	Government organizations, DGs and the tribes
Member	Third Village local Council	very strong	yes	Residents of his Sub-district
Member	Dokem-1 local Council	weak	weak	Residents of his Sub-district

Staff member	Water Directorate in Third Village Sub-district	medium	no	Employees in his directorate
Chairman	Teachers' association in Dokemy	strong	yes	Most teachers of Dokemy District
School principal	Dokemy Elementary school	fairly weak	no	Students and their parents
Professor, Environment	College of Sciences- University of Sadbokan	low	no	Many professors and students
Director	Zefuk Centre for Investment Studies - Sadbokan	medium		Many researchers
Member	Cultural Gathering	weak	no	Many educated people
Physician	Dokemy Hospital	strong	yes	Other doctors
Chairman	Cultural and Sports Center in Third Village Sub-district	medium	yes	Intellectuals and educated people
Chairman	Dokemy Sports Club	strong	no	Young people
Manager	Women office in Third Village Sub-district	very strong	yes	Women
Chairman	Zefuk Disabled people Association in Dokemy	medium	no	Disabled people in Dokemy
Chairman of the Rainforests and Marshlands Committee	Local council in Dokemy	strong	yes	Residents of his Sub-district and Rainforests and Marshlands residents

Head of tribe	Dara tribe	very strong	yes	His tribe and many other tribal leaders in the area
Head of subtribe	Dara tribe	medium	yes	His tribe and many other tribal leaders
Head of Big tribe	Big Tribe	medium	yes	His tribe and other tribal leaders
Cousin of the tribal leader of Beta tribe	Beta tribe	strong	yes	His tribe and other tribal leaders
Head of tribe	Subo Tribe	very strong	yes	His tribe and most of the other tribes
Head of tribe	Hika Tribe in Sadbokan	medium		Many of his followers
Head of tribe	Number 18 Tribe			Many followers
Head of tribe	Number 16 Tribe			Many followers
Head of tribe	Number 17 Tribe			Many followers
Head of tribe	Number 10 Tribe		yes	Thousands of followers
Head of tribe	Number 9 Tribe			Hundreds of followers
Head of tribe	Number 11 Tribe			Hundreds of followers
Religious cleric	Leader 1	strong	no	Majority of population in Dokemy District
Religious cleric	Leader 2	strong	no	Majority of population in Dokemy District
Cleric	Leader in Sadbokan	very strong		Thousands of followers
Manager	Zefuki Industries Union in Dokemy	strong	yes	Many businessmen and local companies

Manager	Construction company	strong	yes	Other contractors
Chairman	Engineering Consultancy Firm in Sadbokan	very strong	yes	Many academic figures, tribes, and politicians
Chairman	Sadbokan Chamber of Commerce	very strong	yes	Many businessmen
Manager	Company # 1	very strong		Influences many other businessmen, politicians. and government senior officials
Manager	Company # 2	very strong		Influences many other businessmen, politicians. and government senior officials
Manager	Company # 3	medium		Influences many contractors
Training coordinator	Froon Fund	strong	yes	Local residents and other NGOs active in the area
Manager	WAWZ Zefuk Society in Sadbokan	medium		Influence many people
Manager	Humanitarian Society - Sadbokan	medium		
Manager	Organization for displaced and emigrants - Sadbokan Branch	medium		
Director	CCO Development Centre -Sadbokan	medium		Other CCOs

Director	Manyl Association - Sadbokan	medium		Women groups
Director	Centre for Investment Studies - Sadbokan	medium		Many researchers
Director	Association for Human Rights - Sadbokan	very strong		Through their relations with people in the area of operation
Director	Rural Woman Society - Sadbokan	medium		Through her relations with women groups
Commander in charge of oil security	Army forces	very strong	no	N/A

OUTPUT # 2

STAKEHOLDERS' EXPECTATIONS AND CONCERNS

The Stakeholder Influence Table, a crucial tool in managing stakeholder engagement, offers a structured approach. While the information it provides is subjective and, in some cases, sensitive, it should be used with caution. Given the potential sensitivity of the information, its distribution should be limited.

Formal interviews were conducted with tens key stakeholders from the District of Dokemy - focusing particularly on the Sub-districts of Third Village and Dokemy City - and from the Rainforests and Marshlands area. The objectives of the interviews were to understand the attitudes towards investment by foreign companies of local leaders and influential people from the populated areas close to the field of Upper Banop.

Overview

Stakeholder interviews were conducted with a diverse range of key leadership representatives and influencers in the District. This included local authorities at the District and Sub-district level, as well as individuals representing specific communities (youth, women, disabled people, Rainforests and Marsh people) or sectors (oil industry, private sector, health sector, education). This comprehensive approach ensures that all perspectives are considered in our findings.

In order to maintain the anonymity of RECUSTAT, all interviews were conducted under the cover story of the CSR team, researching the market for the needs of foreign investment companies, whether linked to the oil industry or not.

Overall, the results of the survey paint a promising picture, indicating a strong receptiveness towards foreign investment in the area. This should instill a sense of optimism and confidence in companies considering investment in the District of Dokemy.

All interviewees expressed a unanimous agreement on the positive impact of foreign companies establishing operations in Zefuk. The potential benefits, including job creation, business growth, infrastructure improvement, and overall local development, should provide a sense of security and confidence in the decision to invest.

Employment and unemployment crosscut nearly all sections (Questions 1,2,4,6,7). Creating employment was mentioned as one of the main development needs, as the most important prospective benefit of foreign investment but also as a key challenge for oil companies. Failing to address this issue or not using the local workforce and local companies were mentioned as a major potential reason for opposition.

Other prospective benefits highlighted by the respondents can be summarized in two groups:

- Investment in Human Capital (Building capacity of the local workforce through training, transfer of foreign skills and modern technologies to "raise the industry to international standards", improved provision of local public services, change in the local attitudes, overcoming isolation of Zefuk and build "openness to the outside world")

- Investment in infrastructure (the respondents mentioned many types of infrastructure, from roads, bridges, and dairy processing plants to "Sports City" and "Entertainment City")

The majority of respondents believe that foreign companies, although they are not responsible for providing public services, should contribute to local development by investing in infrastructure and community development initiatives. According to respondents the priority needs which foreign companies could invest in fall into three categories:

- Improved public utilities such as electricity, water, health, schools, and roads;
- Infrastructure to develop the local economy such as rehabilitation of agriculture and improvement of skilled labor (carpentry and iron works, handicrafts);
- Infrastructure to support social life and community interaction such as sports facilities for the youth and entertainment parks. This category reflects the desires of the community to become a more 'normal' society with access to leisure activities and facilities.

This issue of land acquisition and compensation was clearly stated both as a key risk to foreign companies and as a concern for the local community. Indeed, the impact on farmers and the issue of land confiscation were recurrent themes in our conversations with the stakeholders. It appears from our discussions and findings that farmers may be heavily impacted by RECUSTAT's operations in this mainly rural area. In this context, there is a high probability that farmers, with the support of tribal leaders who manage farmlands, may demonstrate opposition to RECUSTAT if the issue of land acquisition is not well managed. Interviewees who raised this issue also expressed an expectation that foreign companies would be involved in this process to ensure adequate compensation standards are achieved.

Security was repeatedly highlighted as a key challenge for foreign companies and a major concern for the communities. It was also mentioned as a social need. Interviewees especially noted the risk posed by some armed groups involved in violent activities targeting foreign companies. CSR team could not confirm this information without disclosing more information about our intent but given the unstable context and the forthcoming economic development, violent groups still present a challenge for companies like RECUSTAT operating in Zefuk.

Most respondents stated that the community would generally welcome foreign companies but would need to see clear evidence of benefits flowing back to the local population. This highlights the importance to RECUSTAT of communicating clearly and openly about their activities and the benefits that their presence may bring to the community.

The survey results underscore the necessity for RECUSTAT to communicate clearly and openly with the local community. This approach fosters trust, transparency, and a shared understanding of the benefits that RECUSTAT's presence can bring to the community.

The key themes which CSR Team suggests RECUSTAT should focus on are:

1. Building trust through communication

Feedback from stakeholders underscores the crucial role of the local population in RECUSTAT's operations. It is imperative for RECUSTAT to build their trust, establishing a transparent dialogue which involves community information liaison officers, media relations (press center) and stakeholder engagement program (communication, information lunches, forums, etc.). Key considerations to address through communication include the following:

It is important to explain the nature of the contract signed between RECUSTAT and the Zefuki authorities to develop the Upper Banop oil field. Local people have received little objective information about the development of the neighboring oil field. RECUSTAT, as a contractor to the Atukaz Oil Company, will be responsible for the operational aspects of the project, ensuring compliance with environmental and safety regulations, and managing the revenue and profit distribution as per the contract. Emphasizing this role and how the revenues and profits will flow to Zefuk from this contract would help clarify current misunderstandings.

Communicate the potential benefits of the project clearly and regularly to various sections of the community. This is much more than a press conference. It's a constant telling and retelling of the positive impact of investment to the community in ways that are relevant to them. The messages should be nuanced to suite various groups. RECUSTAT must be careful to manage expectations for potential employees, local businesses, and the community generally. For example, people need to understand that while jobs will be created, RECUSTAT's presence alone will not entirely eliminate unemployment.

Explain how RECUSTAT will invest in developing the local community and how they will consult with the community about their priorities.

Use multiple communication mediums – while traditional media is important, many respondents emphasized the need for local coordinators (Zefuki and foreign representatives) to talk directly with key leaders on a regular basis. RECUSTAT must carefully design and quickly establish the right mechanisms.

The Stakeholder Engagement Plan incorporated in this report provides an excellent framework to begin the engagement process. It includes a detailed timeline, key milestones, and the roles of each stakeholder. This plan will guide our efforts to build trust, engage potential opposition groups, understand local decision-making processes, and prepare local businesses and workforce for collaboration.

2. Engage potential opposition groups

Respondents, who mentioned potential opposition from various groups as a challenge for foreign companies, also suggested the need to engage with and even employ members of such groups. This is particularly true of tribal leaders. To address this, RECUSTAT will implement a carefully managed program to employ limited numbers in low level positions. This strategy was recommended by many as the best means to reduce security risks and build trust with these groups.

3. The need to understand and work with local decision making and consultation processes

It is important that RECUSTAT understands the different roles of provincial and district level governments, Governor's office and directorates, tribes and community leaders in decision making and consultation. This is further explained in section 5 and should help RECUSTAT to work through the established Zefuki decision making and consultation processes. This will increase transparency and trust and minimize the risks of alienating sectors of the community.

56

4. Prepare businesses and the workforce to work with RECUSTAT

It will be important for RECUSTAT to explain what opportunities will be available for local businesses to supply goods and services to the project and what types of skilled workers they will need. Furthermore, RECUSTAT should demonstrate a commitment to equipping businesses and workers so that they are at a level required. This will help address concerns raised about potential loss of jobs and negative impacts on local businesses.

List of Interviewees

Mr. Influencer, Deputy-Director of the Municipal Council at Third Village Sub-district

Mr. Influencer, Atukaz Oil Company employee from Dokemy District

Mr. Sheikh Influencer from Dokemy District

Mr. Influencer, Chairman of the Teachers Union in Dokemy District

Mr. Influencer, Director of Youth and Sport Committee in Dokemy District

Mr. Influencer, Chairman of Third Village Sub-district Municipality Council and Mayor of Third Village Sub-district by interim until next municipal council elections

Mr. Influencer, President of the Association for Zefuki Disabled people, Dokemy District

Mr. Influencer, Member of the Board of Directors of the Cultural Assembly,

Mt. Director of Public Relations and Member of the Board of Editors of the Cultural Magazine, Dokemy District

Mr. Influencer, Chairman of the Municipal Council for Dokemy District

Mr. Influencer, Engineer at Atukaz Oil Company, Head of Station 8, Third Village Sub-district

Mr. Influencer, Representative of the Zefuk Union for the Industries - Third Village Sub-district

Mr. Influencer, Official at the Department of Water Resources, Third Village Sub-district

Mr. Influencer, Director of the Committee for the Rainforests and Marshlands in Dokemy District

Ms. Influencer, Coordinator of the Training Department for Froon Fund, Sadbokan

Mr. Influencer, Mayor of Dokemy District

Dr. Influencer, Physician at Dokemy Hospital, Third Village Subdistrict

Mr. Influencer, Member of the Third Village Municipality Council, Third Village Sub-district

Mr. Influencer, Member of the Third Village Municipality Council, Third Village Sub-district

Mr. Influencer, Owner of a Construction Company, Third Village Sub-district

Ms. Influencer, Primary School, Third Village Sub-district

Ms. Influencer, Head of Women's office and Headmistress of Fadosa Secondary School for Girls, Third Village Sub-district

Mr. Influencer, Director of the Cultural and Sports Center at Third Village

Mr. Influencer, Cousin of the Sheikh of Beta tribe, Dokemy District, Rainforests and Marshlands area

Mr. Influencer, General tribal leader of tribe in Zefuk, Dokemy Sub-district

Mr. Influencer, President of Dokemy Sports Club, Dokemy District.

Interview Response Summary

Q 1. Do you consider the involvement and investment of foreign companies (especially the ones related to the oil industry) in Zefuk to generally be: positive, neutral, or negative?

Q 2. Do you expect foreign companies to contribute to the development of the local community?

If yes, in what ways do you expect them to contribute? How would you like them to contribute?

Q 3. Do you see any other benefits foreign companies can bring to this area while establishing operations there?

All interviewees considered that the involvement and investment of foreign companies is "positive" and "useful". However, their answers also reveal expectations of foreign companies.

- Creation of job opportunities which will "eliminate" the unemployment problem and
  "develop un-utilized resources" "for many years to come"

- "Investment will help the region in providing complete social services such as health and education"

- Transfer of industrial development and modern technical expertise, knowledge, and skills to the community "which will allow the community to make a leap forward in terms of international quality", "raise the industry to international standards" "which will combat the isolation of Zefuk" and "will allow Zefuk to keep pace with international development"

- Allow "openness to the outside world"

- Improvement of the economic level of the area and an increase in the "monthly incomes of the population"

- Provision of greater safety and security

- Creation of a favorable and positive environment for further foreign investment

- Provision of entertainment and comfort for the community. "Foreign investment results in useful projects such as Sports City and the Entertainment City"

- Foreign companies will "contribute to the process of reclamation of the agricultural lands"

COMMENTARY:

- The people we interviewed unanimously viewed foreign investment as positive and necessary for Zefuk's economic growth. There are also high expectations amongst the respondents regarding the contribution of foreign investment. Interestingly most of them expect and hope for investments in human capital development and new technologies over investment in infrastructure.

- According to interviewees, foreign investment will create job opportunities and solve the problem of unemployment whether directly or indirectly. Foreign investment will stimulate and increase the provision of public services such as "education and health" which in turn will create job opportunities.

- Many of the interviewees focused their answers on youth. Foreign investment will create job opportunities for the "unemployed young people". The population of the district is relatively young, and the future and employment of younger generations is a priority.
- Some interviewees understand that foreign investment companies will not directly provide public services however many expect foreign companies to contribute to the provision of public services such as electricity, water supply, education, or infrastructure. This issue needs to be particularly well managed as it may become a source of tension.
- 9 out of 26 respondents expected foreign companies to be involved in the process of land reclamation and notably the payment of compensation.

Q 4. Which foreign company working in the region are you aware of?

The majority of the interviewees were not aware of any foreign company working in the region. Only two stakeholders mentioned one international oil major.

COMMENTARY:

RECUSTAT's name was not mentioned at any time during these interviews. It indicates that the local population has little or no knowledge of which the international oil company is developing the Upper Banop oil field.

Q 5. What are your or your community's concerns about foreign companies establishing operations in your region?

- Security and poor behavior by private security companies working for foreign companies

- The militias from neighboring areas who might get involved in contract area as a result of greater foreign economic presence. "These militias target foreign companies" and usually "come from the North"

- Transfer of Western customs to the local population

- With regards to the oil industry, proximity of the oil field to the populated areas and consequently the air pollution from the flares and health impact from this pollution

- Environmental pollution

- Reliance on foreign workforce to do the work which will reduce job and training opportunities for the local youth

- Administrative corruption which will come hand in hand with the investment of foreign companies in the area

- Non-compliance with security requirements which could lead to accidents and pollution.

Eviction of the people from their lands because of the confiscation by the State in the interest of the foreign companies and no alternatives offered to them.

COMMENTARY:

It's noteworthy that a significant 70% of the respondents expressed concerns about foreign companies establishing operations in the area. These concerns, often linked to the development of neighboring oil fields, underscore the potential impact of Oil Majors' activities on the local population and RECUSTAT's expectations.

Security, pollution, reliance on foreign workforce, and land acquisition by foreign companies are the main sources of concerns for the population. It's crucial to emphasize that effective communication and dialogue with local communities are not just important, but essential for RECUSTAT to address these concerns.

RECUSTAT plays a pivotal role in addressing the key challenges that arise from foreign companies' operations. These challenges include managing expectations relating to unemployment and handling the issue of land ownership.

Q 6. Which group might be most affected by foreign companies' activities? Why? How can they be reacted?

• Farmers, who can be reached through the Municipality Council, Farmers' Association, or the Tribal leaders (Sheikhs) to which the lands belong.

• Local companies and contractors because of the competition. These companies can be reached through the Local District Construction Council.

COMMENTARY:

Most of the respondents identified the farmers as the most affected by the operations of foreign companies in the area. The District of Dokemy, a region known for its agricultural economy, is home to many villages whose main source of income is from agriculture. This reference to farmers is no surprise as several respondents predicted that farmers might have their lands confiscated and that this might lead to opposition. However, these respondents also explained that fair compensation to the farmers or the provision with an alternative source of income would minimize the economic impact from the loss of their lands.

40% of the interviewees expressed a positive outlook, stating that they believe most people will benefit from the activities of foreign companies, thereby fostering a sense of optimism about the potential positive impact of these operations.

Q 7. What problems do you think a foreign company can face when operating in this region?

• Resistance from farmers because of the confiscation of their lands without adequate compensations or the impact on their farming activities

• Disputes over land ownership

• Security, particularly gangs from the "North" or "some people who may take advantage of the situation"

• Resistance from local population if local people are not employed

• Tribal conflicts that may arise if foreign company's favor particular tribes over others. Tribal conflicts may arise as some tribes are stronger and more influential than others.

• Corruption and bribery linked to less educated people and "lack of awareness" from rural parts of the population who might "exploit these companies by imposing their protection on them or obliging them to paying tributes".

COMMENTARY:

Security was frequently mentioned as a concern for companies. Interviewers have identified different sources of tension: armed gangs from neighboring places targeting foreign companies; opposition from farmers dispossessed without being compensated; tribal conflicts arising as some tribal leaders try to monopolize job opportunities. One interviewee specifically mentioned the issue of oil pipelines that may pass through lands owned by residents and farmers. People recognize the correlation between unemployment and security issues and believe that as foreign companies create jobs, the security situation will continue to improve.

To manage these challenges, RECUSTAT, a local research and statistics organization, will need to work closely with the local authorities and local security forces, providing data-driven insights and recommendations for effective decision-making.

On the other hand, tribal leaders and local authorities' representatives responded that foreign companies would not face problems while operating in the region.

Q 8. What do you think are the top five needs in your community, and which of those most urgently need to be addressed?

• Electricity (rehabilitation of electricity network and provision of electricity)

• Potable water supply (rehabilitation of water network and provision of potable water)

• Health services (construction of healthcare institutions, provision of medical services, health awareness programs/trainings for women)

• Education (construction of schools, literacy programs for women, opening literacy centers for adults)

• Employment (solving the problem of unemployment, job opportunities for women)

• Infrastructure (pavement/rehabilitation of roads and main streets, building bridges)

• Security

• Youth sport facilities

• Industry and Agriculture rehabilitation

COMMENTARY:

Electricity was mentioned most often as the most significant need which is understandable given the disruption to supply which residents have experienced during summer. Respondents highlighted different aspects of economic growth.

The common understanding is that foreign companies, through their investments in this area, will stimulate the local economy, create job opportunities, and improve public services.

The local authorities will also play a crucial role in ensuring the provision of these services. This needs to be an essential aspect of dialogue with the local population. Most respondents are aware that it is ultimately the government's responsibility to provide public services for the population; however, in their view, the inefficiency and corruption of the government since 2010 means there is little confidence in the government's capabilities and political will to deliver these services. With foreign companies establishing operations in the area, they see an opportunity to get better public services, with the foreign companies somehow indirectly contributing to these. Two respondents clearly stated that only foreign investment has the capacity and knowledge to implement reform with a vision and a plan.

Q 9. Who are the influential stakeholders, including individuals and organizations which foreign companies working in this region must gain the support of?

• Tribal Leaders and their sons (Beta tribe headed by Chieftain Pedro, Dara tribe headed by Sheikh Iba)

• Municipal Council and General Director of Water and Electricity

• Religious Clergy

• Notables/ Dignitaries

• People in charge of Youth and Sports Committee/Club (since it involves more than 5,000 young people)

COMMENTARY:

Most interviewees emphasized that the support of the tribal leaders was as important as the support from the local official authorities (mayor, municipal Council, local DGs). The tribal leaders, being influential figures in the community, can help facilitate the smooth operation of foreign companies by mediating potential conflicts and ensuring the interests of the local population are considered.

Table 3

Tribal leaders (Sheikhs)	23 respondents
Municipal Council/ Mayor/ local DGs	22 respondents
Religious Clergy	3
Notables/ Dignitaries	4
Youth and Sports Club President	2

While endorsing the role of local authorities, responses to this question also highlight the importance of Tribal support. Dokemy District has a large rural community whose first loyalty and identification are tribal. They are very influential in shaping sentiments within the community. This is underscored by the comments of representatives from the local authorities who confirmed the need to consult with and gain the support of tribal leaders in the area.

When foreign companies establish operations, the support of tribes is not just important but crucial for security. The responses to question 7 underline the potential for tribal conflicts if communication and engagement with tribes are not effectively managed, emphasizing the need for robust communication strategies and risk management.

Results of this question vary from those of Sadbokan, where consulting with tribes is considered less critical.

Q10. Which international and national aid organizations have been successful in your region? Why do you think so?

COMMENTARY:

Respondents remembered only a few organizations working in the area in the past. The second question drew very little response.

Froon Fund and Saveaa Fund are working on projects funded by the different Agencies for Social Development. Noting the large number of international organizations that have operated on the ground in the past, it is interesting to see that only a few are recognized and remembered.

Q 11. Which groups, organizations, and community leaders should be consulted when determining which community initiatives should they contribute to?

Dignitaries

Tribal sheikhs

Local elders

Local Construction Council

Members of the Provincial Council

Municipal Council (Mayor, DGs)

Civil Society

Civil organizations working in the region.

COMMENTARY:

According to respondents, consulting and involving public official authorities in defining which community services foreign companies may contribute to is not just beneficial but essential. This response echoes the results of question 8, as stakeholders acknowledge the indispensable role of local authorities in providing public services. RECUSTAT must prioritize consulting and working with the local authorities regarding community initiatives.

Table 4

Stakeholder	Q11 - Respondents
Tribal sheikhs	4 respondents
Elders	2
Dignitaries/Notables	12
Municipal Council (Mayor, DGs)	13
Local Construction Council	5

Provincial Council	1
Civil Society	1
Organizations working in the area	1

If we compare results of Q9 (regarding support and influence) with results of Q11 (who determines community services), it is clear that tribal leaders' consultation and support is key. However, this should not be confused with a decision role which is clearly seen as the responsibility of local authorities.

Table 5

Stakeholder	Q9. Who are the influential stakeholders, including individuals and organizations which foreign companies working in this region must gain the support of?	Q11. Which groups, organizations, and community leaders should be consulted when determining which community initiatives should they contribute to?
Tribal leaders (Sheikhs)	23	4
Municipal Council/ Mayor/ local DGs	22	13
Religious Clergy	3	0

Notables/ Dignitaries	4	12
Youth and Sports Club President	2	0
Elders	0	2
Local Construction Council	0	5
Provincial Council	0	1
Civil Society	0	1

Q12. What is the best way for foreign companies operating in Dokemy District to consult and communicate with the local community about their operations and local community development plans?

- Face-to-face consultations/meetings with representatives of the foreign companies

- Public forums with representatives of the foreign companies which should be advertised in advance

- Questionnaires to be distributed to the communities prior to meetings

Interviewees indicated their preference to have an Zefuki representative of the foreign company together with a foreign spokesperson to make sure that the main ideas and message are not lost in translation.

OUTPUT # 3

POWER BALANCE BETWEEN FORMAL AND INFORMAL STAKEHOLDERS

It is important to understand the distinct decision-making and consultation roles of various parts of government, such as the executive, legislative, and judicial branches, as well as the roles of different community groups, including local residents, business owners, and environmental organizations.

As part of the informal approval process, it is essential to win the support of various groups. This inclusivity is not only a requirement but also a way to ensure that all voices are heard. Additionally, formal approval is necessary from key levels of government, including sub-national local government and national government representatives through line ministries.

It is recommended that prior to the start of any operations and taking into consideration the complexity of the stakeholders identified through this study, that a comprehensive engagement program be developed.

RECUSTAT will need to engage with formal and informal decision-makers at all levels of provincial, district, and sub-district administration.

The main stakeholders will include:

Provincial level

- Provincial Council
- Governor's Office
- Technical Directorates (regional representatives of line ministries from state Capital)

District / sub-district / community level

- District Councils
- Sub-district Councils
- Tribal Councils
- Mayors
- Technical Directorates (not all)
- Religious Clerics
- Local Business
- Local NGOs
- Community Leaders

Security Forces

- Zefuk Army (ZA)
- Police
- Oil Protection Force
- Atukaz Oil Company
- Coast and Border Guards

Oil Protection and Security Forces will play an important role for RECUSTAT field operations and CSR Team advises further analysis of the Oil Protection Force.

Local Government Structure

Roles & Responsibilities of Key stakeholders in the local government

Provincial Council

The Provincial Council (PC) is comprised of committees responsible for various areas such as health, economic development, infrastructure, tribes, district councils, etc. The local Council's Committee and the Oil Committee would be direct contacts in Provincial Councils for RECUSTAT Oil Company.

The PC subcommittees generally act as consultative groups and do not have decision-making authority. Their recommendations are presented to the PC for approval.

Role of the PC in decision-making:

The PC is responsible for developing the Provincial Development Strategy and setting the development priorities and sector budgets of the Province. Based on the allocations of the PC, the Governor's Office develops a Provincial Development Plan (PDP), which is a list of priority projects for a detailed provincial budget for each sector. This is developed in consultation with the relevant technical directorates and is again approved by the Provincial Council. The Provincial Council is expected to ensure that the PDP reflects provincial development priorities outlined in the Provincial Development Strategy. This helps achieve some alignment between the priorities of the Central Government and the priorities of the PC. During the budget development phase, directorates may consult with the relevant PC sub-committees; however, the PC is (or should not be) generally not involved in the detailed spending decisions.

The Governor's office collates the operational budgets of each directorate into an overall Provincial Budget, which is then presented to the Provincial Council for approval. Once the budget is approved, the PC's critical role is to monitor the execution of the budget by the Governor's Office and various directorates.

The Provincial Council plays a significant role in setting policy and determining spending priorities. However, the operational decisions related to each sector are the responsibility of the Governor's Office and individual directorates. The O&M budget is allocated solely to technical directorates through line ministries.

RECUSTAT plays important role in engaging with the PC, especially with the chairs of relevant subcommittees. It is essential to consult with the PC concerning its planned community development initiatives, seeking their input into any community plans. RECUSTAT's proposed investments should align with the PC's policies and priorities. While the PC's support is critical for planning and approval, all operational matters are the responsibility of the Governor's Office and directorates. This underscores RECUSTAT's significant role in the local government structure and stakeholder engagement.

Governor's Office and Technical Directorates

The Governor's Office and Directorates are responsible for the operational management of the Province.

Any donor-funded projects/initiatives that fall under the category of 'core government business' need to be cross-checked with relevant Technical Directorates, which ideally should hold sectoral plans. Formal, written approval of Technical Directorates will be essential for any social investment projects that arise. This is particularly important to minimize duplication of effort and ensure that the Governor's office takes over operational management and any long-term costs associated with the initiative or project.

If the proposed project or investment is not considered core government business, it is still essential to consult with the PC and relevant district council to ensure they are informed and that the project addresses their needs and strategic priorities.

District and subdistrict councils

The district and sub-district councils are also critical consultation and decision-making bodies. Although they currently do not receive any direct funding, the recently passed Law (Provincial Power Act) empowers them to undertake planning and monitoring functions. They are responsible for the provision of some local services and for monitoring implementation by relevant government departments in their district.

RECUSTAT stands to gain significant benefits from effective engagement with district and sub-district bodies. By discussing their needs and seeking their input before deciding which projects/initiatives to fund, RECUSTAT can ensure its investments are well-aligned with local priorities. If proposed projects involve 'core government services,' then formal approval will be required from the district chair, mayor, and relevant directorate. This proactive approach can lead to more successful and impactful initiatives, fostering a positive relationship with the local government and communities.

District and sub-district councils have very strong local representation and links into local communities and tribes. We suggest that RECUSTAT builds strong relationships at the district level.

Key issues

Over the past three years, provinces have received increasing capital funds from the Zefuk Federal Budget, mainly for the acceleration of reconstruction and development. The capacity of the provincial administrations in the Lower South to plan and manage provincial budgets has greatly improved over the past few years. However, the budget execution levels still need to be desired, and achieving a more effective and transparent budget cycle remains at the top of the agenda.

The involvement of the local sub-provincial councils in provincial affairs has been limited mainly to informal engagement; it has yet to be institutionalized. Local Councils often complain of a lack of development opportunities in their communities.

The Zefuki government has already implemented a decentralized budget planning and execution framework for some types of provincial capital expenditures. This framework gives local authorities the responsibility for planning local economic development. Now, under the new Provincial Powers Act, it will be further extended to the sub-provincial level.

The local government structure is evolving, and RECUSTAT is well-positioned to adapt to these changes. The new Provincial Powers Act, which came into effect in 2026, gives authority to the sub-provincial administration's sub-provincial level (district and sub-district) to plan and monitor reconstruction and development activities in their respective areas of responsibility.

The new PPA delegates the following responsibilities to Local Councils:

1. Monitor the progress of the work of the local administration in the districts and sub-districts

2. Prepare draft budgets, including operating budgets, and send them to the Governor

3. Regulate utilization of public land in coordination with the line ministries

4. Assess educational needs and plans to meet them

5. Approve security plans

6. Draft district by-laws.

To exercise these functions successfully, the Local Councils need to work closely with the Provincial Council to clarify each level of local government's respective role and ensure good working relationships.

This new context provides justification and an obligation for the Provincial Council to fully engage the sub-provincial level in the planning process and create a coordination system that will link all levels of the provincial administration. However, the practical implementation of the above is still uncertain, and there are a number of issues pertaining to the empowerment of the districts and sub-districts.

The main problems identified about the sub-national governance:

Strategic Planning:

• Lack of rigorous information baseline to support the identification of strategic priorities: limited access to statistical data, research studies, and field assessments

• Absence of formalized provincial sector strategies combining policy guidelines issued by the Line Ministries and priority needs of the provinces

• Limited participation of districts and sub-districts in the identification and prioritization of development and reconstruction needs

• Ineffective coordination between the Ministry of Development, the Ministry of Finance, and the Administration on Strategic Planning issues and procedures.

Budget Planning & Execution:

• No synchronization of the provincial capital budget with the federal O&M allocations

• Lack of timely and transparent means of communication to share Ministry of Finance Budget instructions with Governor's Offices and Provincial Councils

• Gaps in the technical capacity of the Governor's Offices to perform budget execution functions (i.e., tendering, contracting, project management)

• Absence of standard templates for field assessments, feasibility studies, scope of works/bills of quantities to guide the project design tasks of Technical Directorates

• Gaps in reporting provincial financial statements to MoF with subsequent delays in money transfers.

Sub-provincial level engagement:

• Poor institutional structures for management and planning; the capacities of Local

Councils and Mayor's Offices are limited. There is a lack of well-trained technical staff to

support the elected bodies. Mayor's Offices are not well equipped and not prepared to fulfill their role of monitoring the implementation of the projects.

• Conflicting roles and responsibilities of the key players in districts and sub-districts and a lack of a clear division of labor between legislative and executive; project implementation is with the Technical Directorates, which, ideally, should be coordinated at the district level by the Mayor appointed by the Local Councils.

• Absence of district development strategies; the previous Provincial Development Strategies were prepared with very limited involvement of the district and sub-district authorities. District development strategies do not exist.

• Lack of transparency: local Councils should be accountable to their constituencies; they should be able to communicate with the communities throughout the process of planning and implementation, starting with identifying their needs, presenting proposed solutions (projects/budgets), and implementing them. The current structures do not provide sufficient communication with their constituencies.

• Budget allocation to sub-provincial level: The way provincial budgets will be allocated and planned is not yet defined. The law provides for allocation to the districts and empowers them to plan their budgets independently. However, it is still not clear how the Provincial Council will distribute the provincial budget and to what extent the districts' allocation decisions will be respected by the PC.

• Lack of a formalized vertical coordination structure, the cooperation between district and provincial levels and between district and sub-district is based on informal communications, often driven by personality rather than process. Almost no information flows from the top down. Therefore, the districts frequently contend that they are not aware of the decisions of the provincial authorities and lack information on project implementation.

IMPLICATIONS FOR RECUSTAT

The local governance structure and the process described above have been put in place as a result of 'new' decentralization. The local government, while having the power to make decisions on local matters, also operates within certain constraints set by the national government. Even though the Zefukis have made significant progress to date, it is still a new concept for them. RECUSTAT needs to understand this system with its powers and constraints as the local government will be, apart from the national government structures responsible for the oil sector, a key stakeholder and partner to RECUSTAT on the ground.

The survey results underline the local government, namely local councils, as the key partner for foreign companies working in the region. This underscores the importance of RECUSTAT establishing strong relationships with these stakeholders. Working with and through the local government structure when planning and implementing social investments will be inevitable. However, if not properly understood or managed, it can pose significant challenges to the social acceptance strategy of RECUSTAT.

TRIBES

Tribal traditions remain strong and culturally important to many Zefukis. Particularly in smaller cities and rural areas, especially in the South, many tribal leaders have emerged as intermediaries between the communities and the government. They play a central role in representing the interests of their communities to the government and vice versa. Tribes are regional powerholders and tribal leaders, respected members of Zefuki communities, who often have significant influence.

Even though building relationships with tribes is essential, not only from a security point of view but also to reach out to communities, they should not become the primary stakeholders for RECUSTAT.

In many instances, tribal leaders work closely with local councils or even hold positions with legitimate structures. This is the preferred way of building local consensus and working with tribes.

Tribes around selected locations

Mainly peaceful tribes inhabit the Upper Banop oil field; however, the Kinyanu tribe reportedly has a reputation for involvement in criminal activity and should be carefully managed. The key tribes are:

Beta tribe, headed by Chieftain Pedro;

Dara tribe headed by Sheikh Iba;

Budan tribe headed by Sheikh Hura;

Sinori tribe headed by Sheikh Hama;

Hika tribe headed by Sheikh Anas;

Subo tribe headed by Sheikh Mogy;

Kinyanu tribe headed by Sheikh.

RAINFORESTS AND MARSHLAND AREAS

As Upper Banop is in a rich Rainforests and Marshland environment, managing the sensitive Rainforests and Marshland environment and engaging with Rainforests and Marshland, people will be critical to the success of RECUSTAT's activities.

The Rainforests and Marshes, one of the largest wetland ecosystems on Earth, are not just crucial to intercontinental flyways for migratory birds and support for endangered species. They also sustain freshwater fisheries, adding to their ecological importance. But what truly sets them apart is their outstanding natural resources and their unique contribution to the global perspective of human heritage.

The destruction of the Rainforests and Marshlands and the consequent displacement of their indigenous population is one of the significant humanitarian and environmental challenges facing Zefuk. At the same time the Rainforests and Marshlands central role in the sharing of transboundary water resources and the oil has placed the Rainforests and Marshlands' future among the priorities of the Zefuki Government and the international community.

The entire Rainforests and Marsh community has suffered enormous social and economic upheaval due to the Rainforests and Marshlands' destruction. Concurrent with the Rainforests and Marshlands' drainage, a major campaign by the former Zefuki government was launched in the early 1980s to displace the Rainforests and Marsh people. This campaign, driven by economic and political interests, led to the forced relocation of thousands of indigenous people from their ancestral lands. Unfortunately, no valid census data is available, but the initial Rainforests and Marsh population estimates range from 200,000 to 500,000. In 2020, approximately 100,000 to 200,000 Rainforests and Marsh people were displaced within Zefuk. A further 100,000 had to flee the country and live as refugees, including an estimated 40,000 in Ekulon. Only a small number of the indigenous population (around 10%) is believed to still live in the area, and around 85,000 are nearby. In addition, due to the many internal migrations and re-settlements, non-Rainforests and Marsh communities reside within the Rainforests and Marshland region.

Although tribal identity is essential in the Rainforests and Marsh society, they are ethnically and linguistically homogenous. There are three scenarios of the current settlement and livelihoods:

86

• Rainforests and Marsh people who have continued to live in the Rainforests and Marshlands in the traditional way of life.

• Displaced Rainforests and Marsh people resettled on the margins of the present Rainforests and Marshlands on dry land. Livelihoods consist of mixed agriculture activities and limited Rainforest and marsh exploitation.

• Rainforests and Marsh people who have migrated to towns and cities.

Despite displacement and social exclusion, the Rainforests and Marsh people have shown remarkable resilience. They have managed to maintain a strong level of cohesion, with tribes and sub-tribes typically being resettled together in the same area. Tribal leaders continue to exercise a key leadership role, and the traditional meeting room, a center for the socio-cultural system and a forum for tribal politics, remains a common element of the landscape.

It should be noted that, in the main, the Rainforests and Marsh people do not wish to be treated separately from surrounding host communities. Assistance to the Rainforests and Marsh people and the Rainforests and Marshlands restoration should be integrated within the broader regional and local development framework. This integration can lead to a win-win situation, where the conservation of these ecosystems not only benefits the indigenous people and the environment but also contributes to the overall regional and local development. When asked to identify their medium- and long-term priorities, the older generation usually favors returning to the traditional way of life. In comparison, the younger generation prefers to be engaged in commercial activities and very often remain or move to the urban industrialized areas. In a fully participatory planning process, the needs of local residents should obviously figure prominently, although fitting into a higher-level, longer-term planning framework for the Rainforests and Marshlands.

Even though the federal government's priority is increasing oil production, other considerations (such as the environment) are secondary. This prioritization has led to conflicts with the conservation efforts for the Rainforests and Marshlands, which are recognized globally as essential and fragile historical and environmental sites. The existence of oilfields throughout this area and the potential for further discoveries will likely create significant tension as the Government of Zefuk manages the commercial and environmental/social/historical interests. This tension underscores the need for a balanced approach that takes into account the economic, social, and environmental aspects, ensuring the sustainable development of the region.

The key stakeholders in the Zefuki Rainforests and Marshlands include:

• Central Government ministries and agencies with responsibilities in the southern Rainforests and Marshlands;

• Local government;

• Civil society (universities, NGOs, CSOs, local residents, private sector organizations such as Chambers of Commerce and Industry, etc.); and,

• International donors.

Given the importance of the Rainforests and Marshlands and the informal and somewhat disorganized revitalization that was occurring post-2020, at the hands of local inhabitants and various Ministries (supported by donor funds), the Government of Zefuk established the Ministry of State for the Rainforests and Marshlands. The primary function of the Ministry is to provide oversight and coordination for Rainforests and Marsh restoration activities and to elaborate a comprehensive long-term plan for the development and management of the southern Rainforests and Marshlands.

Despite the commendable efforts of the Rainforests and Marsh people and the informal initiatives to re-flood the dried Rainforests and Marsh areas, about 60-70% of the Western Rainforests and Marshlands have been restored to their original condition. However, the severity of the drought since 2028 has led to the unfortunate drying out of much of the re-flooded Rainforests and Marsh Fady lands, posing a significant challenge to our restoration efforts.

NGOs and CSOs in the Rainforests and Marshlands often act as intermediaries, at times representing local residents, or at least having relatively easy access to them, and also at times acting as implementers or facilitators of donor projects in the Rainforests and Marshlands (some have a very good understanding of local security issues and effective strategies for getting work done on-the ground).

The universities in the area (and some in the Capital City) have research interests in the Rainforests and Marshlands (environmental, social, economic, etc.), and have been important partners in building up the information base for the Rainforests and Marshlands. The most active universities include:

• College of Science for Men and Women, University of Capital City

- Marine Science Centre and College of Science, University of Sadbokan

- College of Education, University of Third City

- College of Pharmacy, College of Science for Women

- College of Science, Zefuki University

Local government (and local people) in the Rainforests and Marshlands have shown their commitment to proper restoration and management of the Rainforests and Marshlands by organizing various coordinating bodies; for example, the Coordinating for the Rainforests and Marshlands became operational by June 2025, with representatives from local councils and tribes (not necessarily with the full knowledge and endorsement from the Central Government). The current coordination status for the Rainforests and Marshlands needs to be clarified. Initially, the main interest of the Coordinating for the Rainforests and Marshlands was to seek funds for its operations and a building and to broker projects that might have political leverage in each of the Governorates.

Central Government involvement in the Rainforests and Marshlands typically includes the following ministries:

- Ministry of Planning;

- Ministry of Education;

- Ministry of Education and Research;

- Ministry of Environment;

- Ministry of Agriculture;

90

- Ministry of Public Works;

- Ministry of Water;

- Ministry of Health;

- Ministry of Labor.

Soon after the re-flooding of the Zefuki Rainforests and Marshlands had started, the Centre for Restoration of the Rainforests and Marshlands, based within the Ministry of Water, was established (September 2023). CRM responded to the initial priority issues in the Rainforests and Marshlands with development of a five-year restoration program and with its basic principles in mind, CRM identified initial priorities, in 2023 and 2024, that were intended to guide all work related to restoration issues in the Rainforests and Marshlands.

These were:

- identifying the newly flooded areas;

- monitoring selected sites through regular collection of water and soil samples;

- monitoring and documenting other aspects of the flooded sites, such as vegetation, people's movement, community feedback, economic activities, etc.;

- enhancing the Ministry of Water knowledge of the conditions at the field level;

- coordinating the actions of other stakeholders;

- supporting national and international organizations with interests in the Rainforests and Marsh restoration process; and,

• engaging local communities and authorities in a constructive dialogue regarding their needs, priorities, and responsibilities.

Restructuring within the Government of Zefuk also reflected this shift from science to human development planning. This was the origin of the Ministry for the Rainforests and Marshlands, which was designated in September 2024 and reports to the Council of Ministers.

The Main Donor working in the Rainforests and Marshlands is the LDxDU Fund, funded by the International Development Agency. Since 2025, several planning initiatives have been relevant to the Rainforests and Marshlands. These include various "Master Plans," as follows:

• CRM's Master Plan for the Southern Rainforests and Marshlands (2024);

• Master Plan for Integrated Water Management (Nature Zefuk, 2025, contributing to the "Life Again" initiative);

• National Water Management Plan – First Phase (Ministry of Water, 2026).

PRIORITIZING STAKEHOLDERS

Stakeholders are defined as those individuals or groups on whom the activities of RECUSTAT will have an impact or who may impact the activities of RECUSTAT. Stakeholders will be affected by the presence of RECUSTAT to different degrees, and - generally - the amount of time and effort that should be devoted to working with various stakeholder groups should be proportional to how closely they are affected by RECUSTAT and how vital their support is to the overall success and image of RECUSTAT.

The stakeholders' influence analysis will determine internal and external communications and strategies for working with different groups of stakeholders. The information below presents approaches/strategies suggested by the CSR Team for applying to different groups of stakeholders.

In the prepared matrix, the CSR Team has identified the key stakeholders at the District level in the current context in Zefuk. These are the main players affected by RECUSTAT's activities or who hold significant influence and should, therefore, be engaged in some way. It's important to note that stakeholders are not static entities, and this matrix should be regularly updated to reflect any changes.

Based on comprehensive stakeholder research in Dokemy District, the CSR Team has prioritized key stakeholder groups using a unique methodology. Instead of a typical 2D model, we have employed a Three-dimensional space (3D) model. This approach allows us to categorize stakeholders not only based on their impact and influence but also on their level of interest. This provides a more nuanced understanding of stakeholder dynamics and a clear basis for our engagement strategies.

OUTPUT # 4

KEY ISSUES AND RISKS OF STAKEHOLDER MANAGEMENT

The following risk table, compiled based on our research and knowledge of the Lower South of Zefuk, is not a risk management strategy but a summary of issues and risks emerging from the CSR Team's research. It primarily focuses on local issues and does not address regional risks, such as the potential for regional conflict, as specialists' best comment on these. There may be other risks known to RECUSTAT that we have not considered here but should be adequately assessed. As the project evolves, it is of utmost importance that a comprehensive risk management strategy is prepared, underlining the criticality of this task.

Table 6

Risk / issue	Potential impact	Management
Security instability Primarily problems caused by radical groups and disaffected tribes however the security situation more generally while greatly improved is still fragile and subject to change	Serious – loss of life and could disrupt operations and prevent access	Consultation and communication with Tribes and local communities Employ small numbers of personnel from areas / tribes where risks are high Invest in community development activities in high-risk areas
Bureaucracy Uncertainty around legislation, regulations and approval processes may delay decision making. For e.g., ambiguous environment approval process	Long delays, cost blowouts	Engage Zefuki to cultivate relationships with all key departments and personnel in order to thoroughly understand and effectively navigate through all key processes

Political uncertainty Changes of key government positions as a result of the national elections causing delays and requiring new relationships and trust to be established	Delays in decision making and approvals	Engage political analyst to maintain relationships with government throughout the provinces and in Capital City and to cultivate relationships with prospective candidates
Historic and or environmental site discovery **Lack of reliable site registration and data will require intensive effort to discover areas at risk** **Likely to attract international scrutiny**	Project delays, costly remedial work reputational risk. Uncertainty re: the requirements of the Ministry of Environment will compound this	Activate EIS process as soon as possible to better understand the scope of the issue and to begin addressing concerns Fund environment protection measures as appropriate Engage with broader community and specialists in the region regarding environmental and historic issues
Corruption	Opposition, legal action, damage to reputation, delays to project due to refusal to compromise on illegal payments to stakeholders	Explain zero tolerance policy upfront Transparent decision making and payment processes

96

Lack of qualified workforce	May need to import qualified staff which will create strong local opposition	Support existing and launch new (as required) vocational training programs to equip staff with skills required Use expat staff to capacity build
Lack of suitable/ qualified suppliers	Poor quality work, cost blowouts, production bottlenecks	Support existing and launch new (as required) local business capacity building programs to 'professionalize' local businesses in preparation for working on the project
Inter and intra government demarcation disputes **Competition between the various levels of government and different departments may frustrate decision making**	Indecision, project delays	Clarify role and build relationships with all key departments and levels of government. Understand and work with Zefuki decision making processes

Land ownership issues	Might slow down the operation and negatively impact RECUSTAT's image Might damage relationships with the communities in extreme cases	Provide advice and best international practices to the central government entities responsible for acquisition and compensation schemes. Prepare Resettlement Action Plan social investment program targeting those most affected or relocated and communicate it to the appropriate groups of stakeholders.
Water Access to water for oil production. Issues raised during consultations with rural communities in the region	Perceived competition for water by locals, especially farmers, may lead to opposition and negative sentiment towards RECUSTAT	Minimize competition for water by extracting from alternative sources (other than river). Communicate with farmers about water requirements and methods to ensure that their water supply would not be depleted.

GENERAL APPROACH

RECUSTAT should quickly engage with the local leaders, the community, and various levels of government. RECUSTAT must build relationships with key decision-makers and influencers and establish communication channels to reach the community more generally. The Stakeholder Engagement

Plan (SEP) is the key mechanism through which this can be done. The SEP is included in section 5 of this report and provides a comprehensive and integrated engagement strategy based on:

• key leader (government and community) engagement through relationship building and

communications

• broad community engagement through media and two-way communications

• use of local decision-making processes and consultation processes

• community investment – supporting the community through investment in community initiatives.

RECUSTAT needs to establish clear criteria to guide its decision-making on projects/initiatives for investment. It should prioritize initiatives/projects that align with one or more of the following:

1. Where there is a demonstrated community need or expressed desire

2. Projects that are underfunded or not likely to be funded in the short term by core government budgets

3. Projects where effective local management of the project or initiative by the government or an NGO is assured

4. Projects that contribute to the development of young people, especially employment

5. Projects that strengthen the business and or workforce supply chain for RECUSTAT

6. Projects that will appease potential opposition from specific groups or regions

7. Projects that assist disadvantaged or disempowered people in groups.

In the longer term, RECUSTAT will need to invest in developing the supply chain and labor market to support its projects. The CSR Team suggests that RECUSTAT launch programs to equip businesses and workers to participate in the supply chain.

OUTPUT # 5

IDENTIFYING CANDIDATES FOR TRIBAL LIAISON ROLE

The identification of a Tribal Liaison or Community Liaison Officer has progressed independently of this report. Candidates' CVs have been provided to RECUSTAT, and interviews have been conducted.

The CVs of the following candidates have been submitted:

Candidate # 1

Candidate #1, who has strong experience with the local authorities in Sadbokan, especially the Provincial Council, and has developed a comprehensive network of relations and a good understanding of the local authorities, holds a Master of Political Relations from Sadbokan Technical Institute.

Candidate # 2

Candidate #2, hailing from the Dokemy district near the Upper Banop field, brings a wealth of local knowledge to the role. His experience in construction engineering and community development projects, particularly his work on environmental and health issues for Zefuk and IZLI International construction companies, further demonstrates his understanding of the community's needs. His proficiency in English is an added advantage.

Candidate # 3

Candidate #3, currently serving as a Capacity-Building Coordinator for Froon Fund, has proven his ability to establish and maintain strong relationships. His interactions with local councils, Sadbokan PC members, Atukaz Oil Company, different Official DGs, Sadbokan University, Sadbokan Technical Institute, Employment Service Centers, and Vocational Training Centers are a testament to his interpersonal skills and network-building capabilities.

His tasks involve:

• Organizing and facilitating workshops and training for government officials at the subdistrict levels

• Supporting community delegates and Local Council members to develop and implement advocacy plans in support of community proposals and needs

• Ensuring media coverage for training events wherever possible.

Candidate # 4

From working with international NGOs in Sadbokan, he has gained good experience and has established a solid network. From 2021 to 2026, he worked as a Project Officer and Communication Officer with child protection programs. In 2026, he worked for an International Medical Company to record and support the IDP (Internally Displaced People) population in the Sadbokan province. Since 2027, he has served as Community Liaison Officer for Froon Fund, leading Action Groups in North, Central, and South Sadbokan, dealing mainly with civilians. Candidate # 4 has also gained substantial experience in the media field, acting as Secretary and Chief

Editor of Al Sadbokan Magazine and Chief Editor for Review Today. Candidate # 4 has been volunteering in the Red Crescent Society from 2022 to the present.

He is proficient in English.

Candidate # 5

He is considerably knowledgeable about the social affairs of the people in his area, their values, traditions, and sufferings. Being from and living in the area, he knows most people in the district, from The North village in the East to Sadbokan in the South. Candidate # 5 can relate effectively to all different tribes in the region. He knows most of the area's VIPs and can easily coordinate with them.

As his father was a tribal leader, Candidate #5 acquired knowledge from him on how to deal with rural tribal people, how to contact them on important matters, how to convince them with new ideas, how to solve their quarrels in conformity with the local traditions and values, and so on.

OUTPUT # 6

EXISTING COMMUNITY DEVELOPMENT INITIATIVES

MAPPING OF NGOs AND THEIR ACTIVITIES

In the years before 2020, Sadbokan Province was marred by neglect and hostility from the central government, and the scars of six wars and one civil war. However, since 2021, the province has been witnessing a steady transformation, thanks to the continuous efforts of Local and International NGOs, and various agencies. These entities have been tirelessly working through various programs to uplift the conditions of the population, demonstrating their unwavering commitment to the province.

The following table showcases the collective strength of International Non-Governmental Organizations (INGOs) and National Non-Governmental Organizations (NNGOs) currently operating in the Sadbokan Province. These NGOs, along with different Humanitarian and Philanthropical Agencies, have been working hand in hand, their combined efforts making a significant impact on the ground. However, this table does not cover the activities of these other agencies.

Table 7

Name	Indicative sectors of activity	International (INGO) or National/Local (NNGO)
Bolliv Refugee Council (BRC)	IDPs, Refugees, Shelter, Income Generation Program	INGO
Pacific Relief Foundation	Education, Health	INGO
International help Association	IDPs, Refugees, Human Rights, Shelter, Health, Protection	INGO
Volunteer Centre (VC)	Health	INGO
Life for Development	Health, Food, Education, IDPs, Refugees, Nutrition, Capacity Building for National NGOS, Orphans & Widows	INGO
Froon Fund	Agriculture and Environment, Education, Capacity Building for National NGOs, Community Mobilization, Conflict Mitigation, Gender	INGO
Good Mood	Nutrition, Agriculture and Environment	INGO
Orino Doctors support	Health	INGO

Kind Hands	DPs, Refugees, Health, Education, Food	INGO
Church Aid	IDPs, Refugees, Shelter, Education, Human Rights, Health, Protection	INGO
People forever	Human Rights	INGO
Save my life	Protection, Human Rights, Education, Education	INGO
Nutrigrain Fund	Food	NNGO
Zefuk Foundation	Education, Human Rights and Refugees	NNGO
Zefuk Association	Human Rights	NNGO
Nature Zefuk	Agriculture and Environment	NNGO
Zefuk for Human Rights	Human rights	NNGO
Zefuk Women Association	Gender	NNGO
Humanitarian Association	Human rights	NNGO
Youth Development Association	Gender & Youth	NNGO

Hersuw Association	Culture & Agriculture	NNGO
Rehabilitation Centre for Victims	Capacity Building, Human Rights, Rehabilitation	NNGO
Association for Woman & Child rights	Gender, Human rights, Women's Rights, Children's Rights	NNGO
Fund for Civil Development	Human Rights, Capacity Building, Income Generation	NNGO
LLPX Association	Human Rights, Women's Rights	NNGO
Association for Culture and Organization	Human Rights, Capacity Building, Human Development	NNGO
New Charity Organization	Human Rights, Women's Rights	NNGO
North Association	Woman's Rights, Children's Rights	NNGO
Organization For Child	Children's Rights	NNGO
Organization for Relief and Development	Human Rights, Capacity	NNGO
Second Humanitarian Organization	Health, Children's Rights, Capacity Building	NNGO
Kids and Teens Association	Children's Rights	NNGO

Health Culture & Social Organization	Health, Capacity Building, Children's Rights	NNGO
Children Rights Association	Environment, Human Rights, Education, Health, Children's Rights	NNGO
After Sunrise Association	Environment, Human Rights, Education, Health, Children's Rights, Income Generation	NNGO
Organization for Women	Children's Rights, Human Rights Women's Rights	NNGO
Dokemy Association	Health, Gender, Human Rights	NNGO
Rainforests and Marshes Population Organization	Human Rights, Capacity Building, Coordination	NNGO
Media Research Association	Media and Research	NNGO
Construction organization for civil society	Gender, Human Rights, Capacity Building, Children's Rights, Coordination	NNGO
Association for Women from Rainforests area	Food, Income Generation, Education	NNGO
Sadbokan Centre For Human Rights	Human Rights, Capacity Building	NNGO
Forum Organization	Human Rights & Sports	NNGO

Bigony Organization for Human Development	Human Rights, Capacity Building	NNGO
Zefuk Woman Rights Organization	Gender, Human Rights, Capacity Building, Women's Rights	NNGO
Sadbokan Deaf and Mute Society	Integration of Deaf and Mute People	NNGO
Blind Association	Integration Blind People	NNGO

INGO's COMMUNITY DEVELOPMENT PROGRAMS IN DOKEMY

The Zefuk Foundation, a local establishment since 2005, has been a champion for democracy, human rights, and civil society in Zefuk. One of its notable initiatives, the Dokemy Education project, was a global endeavor that took flight in 2018 in the Western Rainforests Dokemy District. This unique project not only provided literacy training to illiterate and semiliterate adults but also targeted computer training to small business owners, teachers, and selected IT personnel. It furthered its impact by increasing access to technology for the Dokemy population through the establishment of a computer center and distribution of new computers to selected schools. As a testament to its comprehensive approach, the project also provided a grant for generators and water coolers to the community schools that participated in the project (Rain School, Home School, Best School, My School).

Since 2017, the Froon Fund has been a beacon of hope in Zefuk, responding to emergencies with life-saving aid. Their programs, funded by aid agencies, have provided emergency aid and supplemental food assistance to internally displaced Zefukis. They have also extended emergency micro-grants and distributed food through the charity program. Notably, they have provided emergency assistance to highly vulnerable groups such as woman-headed households, tuberculosis patients, and farmers in remote villages. In Sadbokan, their operations have been instrumental in supplying bottled water to the community and medical supplies to local hospitals, saving countless lives.

In 2025, the Children's Rights Association expanded its horizons into the Sadbokan region, embarking on a transformative journey. In a powerful display of collective action, the association partnered with other NGOs to carry out programs focusing on Child Mental Health. These programs included hosting community seminars and providing access to child psychotherapy. Their efforts also extended to Sanitation Hygiene, where they provided sanitation and safe water through water supply systems such as community water tanks, latrines, hand-washing facilities, bathing areas, and drinking water delivery through water tankers. This collaborative approach, a testament to the power of unity, underscored the potential for meaningful change in the Sadbokan region.

OUTPUT # 7

PRELIMINARY SUGGESTIONS FOR SOCIAL INVESTMENT

OPPORTUNITIES FOR SOCIAL INVESTMENT

Operating in a post-conflict context

Decades of wars, internal conflicts, repressions, displacements, paramilitaries, and social unrest have left behind a legacy of deep social, political, and psychological wounds and a generation of young people who don't know any other life than the struggle for survival.

The interviews have underscored the pressing social risks that RECUSTAT faces in the Upper Banop contract area. These include potential opposition from the local community if expectations are not promptly met or effectively managed, as well as the risk of overburdening the local infrastructure and resources. The CSR Team has taken these risks into account in the proposed projects and has developed strategies to mitigate them. Economic and social stability, along with human security, are vital prerequisites for sustainable development. RECUSTAT, as a key player, has the unique opportunity to integrate social investment and support for the recovery process into its social acceptance strategy, potentially bringing about significant positive change in the Upper Banop contract area.

Preliminary Suggestions for Quick Wins:

These projects, which are designed to deliver immediate and visible benefits, include initiatives such as employment creation, infrastructure rehabilitation, and investment in human capital.

The survey shows that employment creation, infrastructure rehabilitation, and investment in human capital are the top three most frequently mentioned needs and the greatest expected benefits of foreign investment. These initiatives are expected to not only address the immediate needs of the community but also contribute to the long-term development and sustainability of the region. Following RECUSTAT's request to investigate opportunities to invest in Quick Wins, the CSR Team prepared the following proposal based on findings from field interviews and research.

Quick Win projects should be quickly implemented (within six months) to build goodwill and support for further engagement with the community. Quick Win projects allow time to develop a longer-term community development strategy. The best source of ideas for Quick Win projects is the local authorities and community. Given that community research to date has been undertaken anonymously without disclosing the identity of RECUSTAT, the suggestions below must be considered as a starting point to help guide discussions with local communities and authorities.

112

CSR Team's suggestions

The support and agreement of local authorities and the community are not just crucial, but they are the backbone of any Quick Win project. RECUSTAT's success hinges on the active participation and input of the communities, leadership, and local authorities in the District. Their involvement is not just appreciated, but it is essential for the success of these initiatives.

Another issue to consider is government support and approval. The approval of local authorities and a commitment to long-term ownership and maintenance of any infrastructure projects should be a prerequisite. In most cases, the District Mayor and Chair, along with the Director General of any relevant ministry, will need to approve any proposed projects.

CSR Team's research indicates that the local community has high expectations of foreign companies regarding employment and the provision of basic needs (electricity, water, and health). This is in part due to the perceived failure of the government to provide for these needs. However, it is critical that RECUSTAT does not become a replacement or complimentary provider of basic services that are the responsibility of the government. The ongoing management of projects should be transferred to local authorities or an acceptable NGO.

This further emphasizes the need for RECUSTAT to consult with local government and communities to gain support and approval before implementation. RECUSTAT will seek formal agreements with the local authorities and will engage in open and transparent communication with the community to ensure their understanding and support for the proposed projects.

While there is no doubt about the need for improved public services, RECUSTAT is committed to its role and responsibilities. It must be careful about investing in the development of services that are primarily the responsibility of government (such as electricity, health, water, etc.). While RECUSTAT may contribute to improving core services, it must avoid being seen as a substitute funder or provider of government services, ensuring that its actions are in line with its mandate and responsibilities.

If RECUSTAT does decide to provide short-term assistance in areas such as drinking water or health clinics, it should do so in cooperation with the relevant Technical Directorate and on the basis that they will take responsibility for ongoing management. One way to avoid responsibility for infrastructure management is to focus investment on capacity building and training. This includes providing local staff with the necessary skills and knowledge to operate and maintain the infrastructure, as well as training community members on how to use and benefit from the services.

Since the Zefuki government and several donors are already investing substantial funds into electricity, water, and hospitals, the CSR Team would suggest that RECUSTAT only use these sectors in exceptional circumstances. For example, RECUSTAT may choose to upgrade roads (core municipality business) that will be used for construction access or to provide drinking water to rural communities around the areas most impacted by the project. This can be justified based on improving the infrastructure that RECUSTAT requires and providing direct benefits to communities that may be negatively affected by RECUSTAT activities. However, RECUSTAT will only consider such investments if they are not duplicating existing efforts and if they can significantly enhance the quality or reach of the services.

Interviews and desk research have identified priorities for investment based on the views of those consulted. These include improving water supply, enhancing healthcare services, upgrading educational facilities, and promoting sustainable agriculture. The suggestions below provide a foundation for further consultation and discussion with the local community to identify and agree on projects to fund. This is not a definitive list, and the CSR Team suggests that RECUSTAT decides to fund projects once broader communication and consultation have been undertaken.

1) Water project

Access to safe drinking water is a main challenge for the populations of the District of Dokemy. Water for drinking and cooking purposes is usually bought from water tankers. According to the CSR Team's independent study, more than 51% of the population in the District of Dokemy is not connected to the general water network. In rural areas or poor districts, households cannot drink tap water (too salty for consumption and sometimes highly contaminated with pesticide residues), and they are forced to buy drinkable water from the market by filling jerry cans (20 to 30 gallons capacity). Specialist shops sell drinkable water. These shops usually buy and stock water transported by trucks (tankers), bringing the water from the local water treatment and purification plant. The water treatment and purification plants use Reverse Osmosis to filter the water from the river. Each house may have a tank located on the roof, which stocks nonpotable water for domestic use. A small electric motor is generally connected to the tank to provide water pressure.

Rainforests Area water plant:

The RO water plant previously built in the Third Village by an NGO has not been in service as the Department of Water Resources/ Ministry of Water has failed to provide an engineer to run the plant. Some interviewees have raised this issue and expressed hope that this problem will be resolved with the help of foreign investment. Interviewees have suggested that the foreign company train a qualified person to fill this gap. Clearly, this would require discussions with the Ministry of Water Resources.

The water treatment plant in the Marshland Area on the Bigony River:

Some interviewees suggested setting up a small treatment plant to benefit the 60,000-person population of the Marshland Sub-district. The plant would produce water for domestic use.

Past experience:

Some NGOs, such as the Froon Fund and Organization For Child, have built water treatment plants and also organized the distribution of water to residents. These projects have proven to be successful and have helped poor people living in remote areas who could not organize transportation or could not buy water from tankers and shops.

2) Medical services

According to CSR Team findings, access to healthcare in the Northern part of the province of Sadbokan is an issue, and public medical facilities have often needed to be better maintained due to the poor security situation and lack of financial resources. Built more than 50 years ago, many are in sub-standard condition. Public medical facilities in the rural areas covered by the District of Dokemy often consist of immobile caravans spread throughout the District. These caravans provide basic medical services to the immediate surrounding population. It is a pragmatic solution by government authorities to address the shortage of medical infrastructure and a way to reach the communities in rural and/or remote areas. However, the caravans are not considered sufficiently well-equipped or staffed to deal with the medical needs of these populations.

Medical Caravan clinics:

Feedback from interviews suggests that providing three to four high-quality caravans could be a valuable social investment project. Local doctors and medical personnel would run the caravans. RECUSTAT could partner with a health-based aid agency to provide and manage a medical unit. RECUSTAT needs to consult and engage with the relevant local authorities regarding the sustainability of this project.

Public clinic under construction in Third Village Sub-district:

RECUSTAT cannot contribute to the construction costs of the building since it has been funded entirely by the government. However, it might be possible for RECUSTAT to provide training, medical equipment, furniture and/or supplies to the clinic once it is completed.

Past Experience: Orino Doctors' support medical project set up a blood bank at the North Public Hospital in 2024, which is now managed by the hospital's medical Team and administration.

3) Electricity

Electricity was the most often cited need by interviewees. Sadbokan's First Deputy Governor estimates that 80 billion USD is required to improve electricity supply in the province. The lack of electricity is especially unbearable during the summer and rainy periods. While most households are connected to the power grid in the District of Dokemy, electricity supply cannot cover all population needs. Electrical facilities do not guarantee a continuous electricity supply, so households use generators to address shortages. The June 2028 protests of thousands of demonstrators in Sadbokan highlighted the exasperation of Sadbokanis with the lack of an electricity supply. While the provision of electricity is clearly the government's responsibility, RECUSTAT may consider providing electricity to a particular project, such as a water treatment plant.

A large water treatment plant was built in Third Village Sub-district; however, it has not been operating due to the shortage in electricity supply at the intake facility. Unable to address this problem, the authorities built smaller and less energy-consuming water plants as a practical alternative to the Third Village main water plant.

Provision of a generator to Third Village water plant: RECUSTAT may consider providing a 750 KVA generator to the main water plant which is not operating because of a lack of electricity supply. This would help to improve the water supply. RECUSTAT would need to partner with an NGO to ensure sustainability.

Solar street lighting for the main central streets and marketplaces in the Dokemy District: RECUSTAT may consider solar street lighting for the main roads and in marketplaces of the District and Sub-districts. Main central streets are usually 500 meters long, and a streetlamp would be required every 25 to 50 meters. These streetlamps can be imported. Public lighting is a safety issue. Estimated Cost: to be determined

It is essential for RECUSTAT to consult and engage with the relevant local authorities regarding the sustainability of these above projects prior to their implementation. Once they are handed over, local authorities must manage these projects so their ownership and commitment to ongoing management is agreed upon.

4) Other community projects

School bags filled with stationery for students of Dokemy District schools: With the start of the school term around February, RECUSTAT may consider distributing school bags with stationery for the primary school students in Dokemy. CSR Team has estimated a population of 10,000 to 15,000 students for the three sub-districts:

• Dokemy (Centre)

• Dokem-1

• Third Village

Estimated Cost: Each school bag is estimated to cost 10 to 15 USD. Stationery may be bought from local suppliers in Sadbokan.

5) Past Experience:

A Kids and Teens Association education program launched a similar operation in Sadbokan in 2025, and the project was deemed successful.

Desktop computers for primary schools: Several interviewees focused on education of young people and have expressed their eagerness for the younger generation to catch up with modern knowledge and technology after years of isolation. RECUSTAT may consider providing computers and training to several schools.

Recreational park: Dokemy District needs a recreational park. This could be a potential area for investment by RECUSTAT. The preferred park location would be Third Village District (at the border between Rainforests and marshes).

Women, children, and youth are among the most vulnerable groups in Zefuk. CSR Team suggests that RECUSTAT give particular attention to these vulnerable groups and aim to implement some Quick Wins community projects to help develop these populations.

Beginning the Early Results initiatives

Given RECUSTAT's limited level of consultation and engagement with the local population and authorities, the CSR Team suggests that the most immediate need is to meet with relevant community leaders to discuss their concerns and opportunities for limited social investment. The community should be asked to prepare a list of potential projects to fund based on some guidelines that RECUSTAT can provide. This will be a key tool to help manage expectations.

OUTPUT # 8

INFORMATION ABOUT THE WORLD HERITAGE

SITES EXISTING WITHIN UPPER BANOP

The stakeholders interviewed indicated that there was no archaeological site in the area of Upper Banop; however, they mentioned the existence of religious shrines considered pilgrimage sites, sites of ancient Indians and indigenous people, such as the shrine of Chieftain Aimas, the shrine of the Shaman Chaws and the Hill of Magic Lide, located to the west of the Dokemy area. The CSR Team met with the Head of the Department of Archaeology in Sadbokan, who warmly invited the CSR Team to provide an official letter and grid references, expressing a keen interest in receiving further information on any archaeological sites of interest in the District.

OUTPUT # 9

STAKEHOLDER ENGAGEMENT AND COMMUNICATION PLAN

STAKEHOLDER ENGAGEMENT PLAN

The stakeholder engagement plan takes the information learned from initial field research and interviews to form a step-by-step action list of engagement activities. The plan is designed to:

• Engage the key stakeholders (determined by the stakeholder mapping).

• Disclose the information relevant to their interests (determined by the stakeholder analysis process).

• Use mechanisms deemed most appropriate to the information requirements of the stakeholder.

Stakeholder consultation should be conducted in accordance with national and international standards and guidelines. Due to the absence of national standards and guidelines in Zefuk, international guidelines create an ethical framework in which RECUSTAT may operate that will remain secure in the face of international scrutiny. This section provides advice relating to stakeholder engagement before the seismic

122

study in the Upper Banop oil field, followed by details of the consultation activities required for the project's life.

Stakeholder Consultation Before Seismic Study

The commencement of seismic activities without adequate stakeholder consultation and completion of the resettlement guidelines is a potential high risk. To mitigate this, a series of early engagement activities are outlined in this section, which are not just minimum requirements but also a 'stop-gap' measure. They are designed to ensure that even if the seismic study prevents a more thorough process of preparation and consultation, the stakeholder engagement process remains comprehensive and effective, thereby ensuring the security and trust of all involved.

The key stakeholders specific to the seismic survey are: RECUSTAT team, Atukaz Oil State Company, local tribal and community leaders, Dokemy district authorities, residents, farmers, and landholders in the Upper Banop Contract Area.

• Atukaz Oil State Company and the Government of Zefuk:

Contractually, responsibility for land acquisition, compensation, and resettlement relating to the development of the Upper Banop oil field resides with Atukaz Oil State Company. However, it is unclear whether Atukaz Oil State Company currently has the capacity or the experience to design, forward-plan, and enact involuntary resettlement to international standards. The application of anything less than international standards is likely to impact the stakeholder environment in which the project is developed. It may result in delays to the development schedule, safety and security issues, and the reputation of RECUSTAT, its development partners, and all international oil companies operating in Zefuk. Therefore, RECUSTAT must support and engage Atukaz Oil State

123

Company in its early engagement activities specific to the seismic survey.

• Local tribal and community leaders:

Knowledge from the preliminary stakeholder study findings indicates that tribal leaders are essential to engage on matters of local significance.

• Dokemy district authorities:

The engagement of local authorities at the subdistrict and district levels will assist in a broader understanding of the proposed seismic survey and will assist in the event the services of some of the authorities are required during or after the program (i.e., for law enforcement, emergency services, etc.). Their involvement ensures that the project aligns with local regulations and that the necessary support is available when needed.

• Residents, farmers, and landholders:

The residents and users of the land within the Upper Banop Contract Area must be consulted prior to the commencement of the seismic survey. It is recommended that they be consulted as soon as possible and again just a few days before the commencement of the seismic survey. Their input is fundamental for understanding the local context, potential impacts, and for ensuring that their rights and interests are respected throughout the project.

Table 8 sets out stakeholder engagement actions specific to the seismic survey. These actions include community meetings, one-on-one consultations, and information dissemination through various channels. In accordance with this stakeholder engagement plan, ongoing stakeholder engagement should continue concurrent with and following these actions for the life of the project.

Table 8

Action plan for stakeholder engagement prior to seismic survey

1.1. Stakeholder

Government of Zefuk

Ministry of Natural Resources

Ministry of Environment

Ministry of Water Resources

Ministry of Health

Ministry of Agriculture

1.2. Engagement mechanism

1. Distribute the project information sheet before the interview. This sheet contains key details about the Upper Banop field development project, including its objectives, timeline, potential impacts, and proposed mitigation measures. Its purpose is to ensure that all stakeholders have access to the same information, promoting transparency and understanding.

2. Conduct a collaborative meeting between a senior representative from RECUSTAT, Atukaz State Oil Company, and relevant national ministers to discuss the following:

- Proposed timing for conduct of the seismic survey

- Likely impacts of the seismic survey on persons who might be economically or physically displaced by the activity

- RECUSTAT's objectives to avoid, where possible, involuntary resettlement and/or minimize the physical and economic impact of its activities

- RECUSTAT's objective is to conduct its activities in accordance with international standards

- RECUSTAT's proposed actions to conduct limited consultation and to prepare a preliminary resettlement guideline, compensation framework, and contractor procedure for land access. This consultation process will involve open discussions, feedback collection, and consideration of stakeholder concerns. The aim is to ensure that all voices are heard and taken into account among stakeholders.

2.1. Stakeholder

Dokemy District authorities:

Governor of Sadbokan Province

Chair of Provincial Council

Head of Municipal Council

District Mayor

Member of Provincial Council

Member of Provincial Council

Chairman of the Council in Dokemy District

2.2. Engagement mechanism

1. Distribute the project information sheet prior to the interview

2.2. Conduct a meeting between a senior representative from RECUSTAT and district authorities, emphasizing the importance of their input, to discuss the following:

- Introduction to RECUSTAT and planned Upper Banop field development

- Proposed timing for conduct of the seismic survey

- Affected area for seismic activity

- Likely impacts of the seismic survey on persons who might be economically or physically displaced by the activity

- RECUSTAT's proposed actions to conduct limited consultation and to prepare a preliminary resettlement guideline and contractor procedure for land access

3.1. Stakeholder

Tribal leaders:

Chieftain Pedro, Head of Beta tribe, the biggest in the area

Leader Diono, Hunaky Tribe

Great Leader Chuool, Vanuul Tribe

Sheikh Iba, Head of Dara tribe

Sheikh Hura, Head of Budan tribe

Leaders of Sinori, Hika, Subo tribes

Religious leaders

Five to ten community leaders or influencers from Dokemy district, comprising active and influential members of communities (other than local government and tribal leaders) such as local entrepreneurs, business owners, academics, teachers, or doctors

3.2. Engagement mechanism

1. Distribute the project information sheet prior to the interview

2. Conduct a meeting between RECUSTAT community engagement staff and tribal leaders to discuss the following:

- Introduction to RECUSTAT and planned Upper Banop field development. RECUSTAT is the lead organization responsible for the development of the Upper Banop field. Our role is to ensure that the project is implemented in a safe, sustainable, and socially responsible manner, with the least possible impact on the environment and the community.

- Proposed timing for conduct of the seismic survey

- Affected area for seismic activity

128

- Likely impacts of the seismic survey on persons who might be economically or physically displaced by the activity

- Proposed compensation framework.

- RECUSTAT's proposed actions to conduct limited consultation and to prepare a preliminary resettlement guideline and contractor procedure for land access

- The importance of community leader support for the development of the oil field

4.1. Stakeholder

Representatives of community organizations:

Chairman of the Youth and Sport Committee

Chairman of Zefuki Industries Union

Chairman of Cultural Gathering Association in Dokemy

Head of Handicap Association in Dokemy.

Chairman of the Teachers' Association in Dokemy

Chairman of Dokemy Sport Club

Selected farmers from Dokemy district (at least one landowner and one lessee)

Ministry of Finance representative authorities responsible for the land registration

Representative of the local farmers' association

4.2. Engagement mechanism

1. Distribute the project information sheet prior to the interview

2. Conduct an initial meeting between RECUSTAT community engagement staff and local landholders and farmers to discuss:

- Introduction to RECUSTAT and planned Upper Banop oil field development

- Proposed timing for conduct of the seismic survey

- Affected area for seismic activity

- Likely impacts of the seismic survey on persons who might be economically or physically displaced by the activity

- Proposed compensation framework

- What they can expect to happen before and during the seismic survey

Conduct a second meeting to notify residents and land users of the imminent commencement of the program, answer any residual questions, and prepare the inventory of existing land use and infrastructure. The purpose of this meeting is to provide a final opportunity for stakeholders to voice their concerns, clarify any remaining doubts, and ensure that all necessary information is collected for the project planning and implementation.

Ongoing Stakeholder Engagement

A regular system of ongoing engagement will be put in place to promote harmonious stakeholder relations across all stakeholder cohorts throughout the life of the project. These ongoing engagement activities should begin immediately and continue throughout the seismic survey, ESHIA process, project construction and operations until the operations close or RECUSTAT 's involvement in the project ends. RECUSTAT should provide consistent, regular information to all relevant communities and clearly demonstrate how issues are followed up between consultation events.

The purpose of stakeholder engagement throughout the life of the project is to:

- Keep stakeholders informed of the project progress and update them with any relevant changes.

- Seek feedback from stakeholders, in particular their concerns or information regarding unforeseen impacts or inadequate mitigation measures.

- Monitor stakeholder attitudes to the project and identify potential issues before they become major problems.

- Seek stakeholder input on how any project-related issues can be addressed.

- Answer stakeholder questions and provide feedback to stakeholders regarding how RECUSTAT is addressing their concerns.

- Reinforce the grievance or feedback mechanism in place for stakeholders.

- Inform stakeholders of the next opportunity for consultation.

Table 9 sets out ongoing stakeholder engagement actions throughout the life of the project, from the seismic study to the end of RECUSTAT's involvement in the project.

Table 9

Action plan for ongoing stakeholder engagement

Stakeholder

Government of Zefuk
Ministry of Natural Resources
Ministry of Environment
Ministry of Water Resources
Ministry of Health
Ministry of Agriculture

Engagement mechanism

1. Conduct regular, quarterly meetings between RECUSTAT management, Atukaz State Oil Company and other Zefuk government ministries plus other International Oil Companies management throughout life of project
2. Monitor feedback and provide responses as required
3. Keep ongoing records of all consultation

Stakeholder

Dokemy District authorities:

Governor of Sadbokan Province
Chair of Provincial Council
Head of Municipal Council
District Mayor
Member of Provincial Council
Member of Provincial Council
Chairman of the Council in Dokemy District

Engagement mechanism

1. Conduct regular, quarterly meetings between a senior member of RECUSTAT and local leaders to provide project updates, obtain feedback, answer questions and monitor potential issues throughout life of project
2. Conduct focus groups on specific issues scheduled if needed
3. Invite feedback via feedback box, phone line and email address
4. Monitor feedback and provide responses as required
5. Keep ongoing records of all consultation

Stakeholder

Tribal leaders:
Sheikh Pedro, Head of Beta tribe, biggest in the area
Leader Diono, Hunaky Tribe
Great Leader Chuool, Vanuul Tribe
Sheikh Iba, Head of Dara tribe

Sheikh Hura, Head of Budan tribe
Leaders of Sinori, Hika, Subo tribes
Religious leaders

Five to ten community leaders or influencers from Dokemy district, comprising active and influential members of communities (other than local government and tribal leaders) such as local entrepreneurs, business owners, academics, teachers, or doctors

Engagement mechanism
1. Appoint dedicated RECUSTAT community engagement staff
2. Establish a community consultation committee
3. Conduct regular, quarterly meetings between relevant RECUSTAT community engagement staff and community leaders to provide project updates, obtain feedback, answer questions and monitor potential issues throughout life of project
4. Conduct focus groups on specific issues scheduled if needed
5. Provide community noticeboards and update regularly with project information
6. Invite feedback via feedback box, phone line and email address
7. Monitor feedback and provide responses as required
8. Keep ongoing records of all consultation

Stakeholder

Representatives of community organizations:
Chairman of the Youth and Sport Committee
Chairman of Zefuki Industries Union
Chairman of Cultural Gathering Association in Dokemy

Head of Handicap Association in Dokemy.
Chairman of the Teachers' Association in Dokemy
Chairman of Dokemy Sport Club
Selected farmers from Dokemy district (at least one landowner and one lessee)
Ministry of Finance representative authorities responsible for the land registration
Representative of the local farmers association

Engagement mechanism
1. Appoint dedicated RECUSTAT community engagement staff
2. Establish a community consultation committee
3. Conduct regular, quarterly meetings between relevant RECUSTAT community engagement staff and community leaders to provide project updates, obtain feedback, answer questions and monitor potential issues throughout life of project
4. Conduct focus groups on specific issues scheduled if needed
5. Provide community noticeboards and update regularly with project information
6. Invite feedback via feedback box, phone line and email address
7. Monitor feedback and provide responses as required
8. Keep ongoing records of all consultation
9. Conduct monthly meetings to notify residents and land users of the imminent commencement of the program, to answer any residual questions and to prepare the inventory of existing land use and infrastructure

Stakeholder

Security organizations:
Zefuki Security Forces
Zefuki Army in charge of securing the area
Army officer in charge of the security of oil companies
Private security providers
Police battalion in charge of securing the area

Engagement mechanism

1. Provide monthly briefing RECUSTAT and other IOC management and representatives of security forces representatives throughout life of project
2. Conduct weekly meetings between RECUSTAT management and security contractors throughout life of project, including other IOC representatives as required
3. Monitor feedback and provide responses as required
4. Keep ongoing records of all consultation

Stakeholder

Women

Five to ten women activists from or around the area (social/human rights/community services)

Vulnerable groups

Internally displaced people
Unemployed
Disabled
Youth
Elderly
Uneducated people

Two to three representatives from each Marshlands village located in the impacted area
Two to three representatives from each Rainforests village located in the impacted area

Engagement mechanism

1. Appoint dedicated RECUSTAT community engagement staff
2. Involve women in a community consultation committee, if possible
3. Conduct regular, quarterly meetings between relevant RECUSTAT community engagement staff and women leaders to provide project updates, obtain feedback, answer questions and monitor potential issues throughout life of project
4. Conduct focus groups on specific issues scheduled if needed
5. Provide community noticeboards and update regularly with project information
6. Invite feedback via feedback box, phone line and email address
7. Monitor feedback and provide responses as required
8. Keep ongoing records of all consultation
9. Involve representatives of vulnerable groups in a community consultation committee, if possible
10. Conduct regular, quarterly meetings between relevant RECUSTAT community engagement staff and representatives of vulnerable groups to provide project updates, obtain feedback, answer questions and monitor potential issues throughout life of project

Stakeholder

Representatives of Non-government organization

Intergovernmental Organizations

Environmental NGOs

Development and Human Rights NGOs

Engagement mechanism

1. Appoint dedicated RECUSTAT community engagement staff
2. Conduct meetings between relevant intergovernmental officials, relevant NGOs, and RECUSTAT community engagement staff as required throughout life of project
3. Monitor feedback and provide responses as required
4. Keep ongoing records of all consultation

Stakeholder

Local residents, farmers, landholders

Selected farmers from Dokemy district (at least one landowner and one lessee)

Ministry of Finance representative (as land owned mainly by Ministry of Finance)

Representative of district authorities responsible for the land registration

Agriculture industry group

Representative of the local farmers association

Engagement mechanism

1. Appoint dedicated RECUSTAT community engagement staff
2. Conduct meetings between relevant farmers and landholders, and RECUSTAT community engagement staff as required throughout life of project
3. Monitor feedback and provide responses as required
4. Keep ongoing records of all consultation

Key Messages

Key messages are not just for contractors but also for internal clarity within RECUSTAT. They are designed to be used as a reference when questions about the project are asked. It's important to keep the number of key messages to a minimum, ideally no more than seven, to ensure their effectiveness. These key messages should be consistently communicated throughout all project stages, from the seismic survey and ESHIA to broader ongoing engagement activities for the project's duration. The key messages determined from the stakeholder analysis for initial stakeholder engagement are:

1. RECUSTAT is the contractor and operator for the project, responsible for its day-to-day operations. Atukaz State Oil Company, on the other hand, is the owner of the project, holding the rights to the oil extraction and overall project management.

a. RECUSTAT does not own the oil extracted.

2. RECUSTAT is committed to adequately assessing the project's potential impacts.

a. RECUSTAT aims to meet international standards and best practices for environmental and social performance.

b. RECUSTAT is serious about protecting local interests because local support for the project will benefit the project (without raising community expectations of project-related benefits to the community).

3. RECUSTAT is a commercial concern, not an aid agency.

a. RECUSTAT's primary obligation is to make money for its shareholders.

b. RECUSTAT also recognizes a responsibility to its host community. This responsibility is not yet defined clearly.

c. Project benefits will be the long-term benefits of increased economic activity.

d. RECUSTAT can encourage the government to spend funds in the local community.

4. RECUSTAT will employ local people and procure from local businesses, where practicable, but will need to bring some skilled workers and goods from outside the area.

5. Employment opportunities are real but limited.

6. Not all the specific skills, goods, and services needed for the project are currently available locally. However, RECUSTAT is committed to working with local businesses and communities to identify opportunities for local procurement and employment.

7. RECUSTAT is dedicated to increasing the level of local employment and procurement over time and will provide

training and assistance to local individuals and businesses, aiming to create a sustainable economic impact in the community.

8. RECUSTAT will have a transparent process for selecting employees.

9. RECUSTAT encourages the participation of women, disabled people, and minority groups in the workforce.

In addition, The Stakeholder Study and Mapping should give RECUSTAT a thorough understanding of ongoing or future community development initiatives and groups involved in such initiatives, allowing it to develop an effective social investment plan.

RECUSTAT is committed to investing effectively in community development initiatives that benefit local stakeholders and increase the sustainability of the long-term operations conducted for the Upper Banop project. RECUSTAT understands that land acquisition and potential resettlement issues are significant and will have a material impact on the project. Therefore, these issues must form an integral part of RECUSTAT's stakeholder management, and it has to be dedicated to addressing them in a fair and transparent manner.

Stakeholder mapping and engagement are critical to the success of any multinational planning operations in Zefuk, especially in the country's post-conflict transition. The presence of a multinational company, especially in the case of significant oil exploration projects, can be alienating or intimidating, and local groups seek respect for their contributions to their society. RECUSTAT is committed to navigating the map of local stakeholders and engaging with them in ways that lead to productive relationships for both sides. RECUSTAT aims to forge alliances that build support and awareness and recommend ways to maintain positive engagement in the future.

RECUSTAT Oil Company has to conduct a tailored stakeholder engagement based on the International Finance Corporation's Guidelines for Stakeholder Engagement. Stakeholder engagement is a two-way street. It is essential to be transparent with stakeholders about the project and listen to them as they express their concerns. Company disclosure is both a helpful end and a part of an ongoing consultation process. Stakeholders can play a valuable role in identifying existing conflicts and flashpoints that could be sources of conflict. RECUSTAT will use various participatory tools to ensure that stakeholder voices are heard. Such tools include interviews, community meetings, focus groups, and written submissions. The key to participatory research is dialogue.

Sample questions to assist the field research in identifying each stakeholder's interests, motivations, and position toward RECUSTAT's operations are listed below:

- What is the nature of their interest in oil operations in the local area? Is this interest positive or negative?

- What are their motivations?

- What is their current opinion of RECUSTAT's contractors and subcontractors?

- How is each group positively or negatively affected by the political, economic, social, and security environment in the local area?

- What are the relations among and between groups?

- Are there conflicting interests?

- What promises have already been made to them? How have these promises been recorded?

Drawing on the information gathered in the Stakeholder Study, the next step is to outline a stakeholder strategy that will allow RECUSTAT to identify which stakeholders should be managed most closely and prioritized. It may be helpful to do this by plotting each stakeholder on an influence-interest matrix.

Chapter 3

LAND LAW
FRAMEWORK

SUMMARY OF LAND OWNERSHIP

In modern Zefuk, almost all arable lands, about 96%, and all oil-producing lands are owned by the government. A significant portion of these government lands are administered privately through unique ownership structures. Most occupied lands are state-owned properties, where the government has granted limited occupation rights. The type and extent of these rights determine the estate or interest in the property, providing a clear and distinct understanding. For instance, government lands where the occupier has been given a "life estate" are known as Usenuk lands, while lands equivalent to a leasehold are called Arenuk lands. Currently, in Zefuk, there are four estates in property: • Freehold Estate (Private Ownership)

- The Right of Usenuk (pre-1927)

- The Right of Usenuk (post-1927)

- The Right of Arenuk

When acquiring property in Zefuk, either voluntarily or through eminent domain, the government must acquire one of these four estates in order to obtain clear title to the property.

Estates in property in Zefuk

1. Private Ownership

In the world, the most significant possible estate in land, where the owner has the right to use it, exclusively possess it, dispose of it by sale, and take its fruits, is called a freehold estate or fee simple absolute. So, in Zefuk, this private property is the highest form of ownership. A simple fee represents absolute land ownership; therefore, the owner may do whatever he chooses with the land. When the landowner dies, the land descends to his heirs.

2. The Right of Usenuk (pre-1927)

Before 1927, the Right of Usenuk was the highest form of estate. The Right of Usenuk (before 1927) was an interest in a property in which the government held the fee but granted an interest in the property to the "Grantee." Ostensibly, the Right of Usenuk (before 1927) was equivalent to a leasehold estate. The Grantee could sell, lease, or mortgage the right; however, the government always held the underlying fee. The government could terminate the Right of Usenuk at any time; however, they had to compensate the Grantee in an amount equal to the total fee value of the property.

146

In exchange for the Right of Usenuk (before 1927), the Grantee agreed that he, his heirs, successors, and assigns would pay taxes on the property yearly. The Rights of Usenuk (before 1927) were inheritable—the Rights of Usenuk could (and often were) be passed down from generation to generation. The highest bidder determined the amount of the taxes on Usenuk lands. Each year, the Grantee would pre-pay his taxes; however, if the government received a higher, more competitive bid, the Grantee would be given the right of first refusal. If the Grantee could not pay the new bid amount, the Right of Usenuk would go to the new bidder, and the old Grantee would be ejected. If no competitive bids were received, the Grantee would continue in occupation in perpetuity (so long as the taxes were pre-paid).

Because of their inheritability, there are many tracts of land in modern Zefuk that fall under the pre-1927 Right of Usenuk (although the taxation issue has succumbed to an assessment by the tax authority and is no longer threatened by the highest bidder). The Ministry of Agriculture administers all Usenuk and Arenuk lands.

3. The Right of Usenuk (post-1927)

In 1927, the Right of Usenuk underwent a significant transformation in a pivotal moment in property law history. This was brought about by Law, which effectively reduced the estate of Usenuk. The amendment had far-reaching implications: the Right of Usenuk, once inheritable and subject to the highest bidder, was no longer so. Instead, it became a life estate in the property, contingent upon the payment of taxes determined by the tax authority.

4. The Right of Arenuk

As opposed to the Right of Usenuk (pre-1927), the Right of Arenuk is a significantly lesser estate; however, juxtaposed to

147

the Right of Usenuk (post-1927), the Right of Arenuk is a marginally higher estate in that it is perpetual. The Right of Arenuk is a leasehold estate that can be held perpetually. However, the leasehold estate is burdened by a covenant restricting the land exclusively to the uses specified by the government in the original grant - e.g., agricultural uses, industrial uses, etc. The Right of Arenuk can be sold, leased, or mortgaged. The government can terminate the Right of Arenuk at any time; however, they must pay compensation (see Section 3). In exchange for the Right of Arenuk, the Grantee agrees that he, his heirs, successors, and assigns will pay 10% of the profits generated by the property in perpetuity to the government.

Although the Right of Arenuk is reminiscent of a sharecropper agreement, it is more akin to a crop-fixed rent contract as the Grantee is interested in the property's legal estate. The Right of Arenuk has the benefit of protecting the Grantee's tenancy against adverse incidents. For example, in a drought or flood, the Grantee may pay the government nothing if the land does not produce crops. However, the Grantee has very limited land use rights in exchange for this benefit. If the property's designated use is agricultural and oil is discovered on the land, the Grantee may not extract the oil; his use is limited solely to agriculture.

5. Leasehold Estate

The Land Reform Law was adopted on November 10, 1961. The law provided for the expropriation of 78 percent of all privately owned arable land.

The Land Reform Law, enacted on November 10, 1961, was a testament to the government's commitment to social justice. It aimed to curtail the vast land holdings of the privileged few and redistribute the land through state leases or communal cooperatives. The law set a limit on the maximum amount of agricultural land an individual could own, ensuring a more equitable distribution. By 1969, about 4.2 million acres had been expropriated, and 1.5 million acres had been redistributed to more than 380,000 families. The redistributed lands, while not titled as private property, were titled in the Government of Zefuk, ensuring their rightful use for the benefit of the people.

In 1969, the Land Reform Law was amended. The new law included most of the provisions of the old law but added several new aspects. For example, the maximum an individual could own was further reduced depending upon the crop grown on the land. Holdings above the maximum were expropriated with compensation only for actual improvements such as buildings, pumps, and trees. There was no compensation for the confiscated land itself.

In 1980, another Land Law was implemented. Under the provisions of that act, Zefukis or other nationals, acting individually or in companies, could apply to lease land from the Ministry of Agriculture for a period of not less than five years or more than 20 years (no land could be leased to companies in Capital City). Leases could be renewed in 5-year increments. If the government needed the land, compensation would be paid by law. Law Article states, "For the sake of public interest, the Minister may issue a decision to end the lease and recover the land and to compensate the tenant for the damages he suffered." Further, of the same Article states, "The Minister of Agriculture may establish a committee to assess the value of the trees and facilities and the amount of compensation set forth in the preceding paragraphs under the Head of Land Registration..." Finally, the law provides that the lessee has the right to object to any decision by the Minister of Agriculture so long as the lessee appeals to the Court of the First Instance within seven days of the land's seizure.

6. Indigenous Peoples

Indigenous tribes, particularly those in Rainforests and Marshes, often have villages and towns on government property and usually occupy the land without formal legal interest. While there is no compensable estate at law, custom (and specific government regulations) provide crucial protections to these tribal peoples, respecting their unique relationship with the land. It's important to note that if the tribes are nomadic, there are no protections in customs or regulations to safeguard their interests, highlighting the need for further consideration and protection.

Methods for Land Acquisition by the Government

The key law governing land acquisition in Zefuk is Land Acquisition Law of 1988. That law identifies three methods of land acquisition: Consensual Acquisition, Judicial Acquisition, and Administrative Acquisition.

Consensual acquisition, one of the methods of land acquisition, is an agreement between a government department entitled by law to own property and the owner of a property for the voluntary sale of land. The value of the land is assessed by an independent inspection committee, ensuring a fair and transparent process. It's important to note that the landowner does not know the value offered when he agrees to a consensual acquisition. Still, both the landowner and the government agree to the valuation process. This process, guided by the real estate value assessment law, ensures a just and equitable transaction.

Judicial acquisition is the government taking of property by expropriation or eminent domain. In a judicial acquisition, the court will examine three issues:

• Is the purpose for which the government is taking the property a legitimate public interest?

• Is the subject property reasonably necessary for the project for which it is being acquired?

• Is the compensation that is being offered fair and just?

Administrative acquisition is property transfer between two governmental entities (i.e., between the provincial government and a ministry).

PROCEDURES FOR CONSENSUAL ACQUISITION

The procedures for consensual acquisition are straightforward and ensure that all parties are well-informed. The landowner and the government entity sign a contract agreeing to be bound by having an independent real estate committee determine the property's value. At the request of the purchasing entity, an independent inspection committee is appointed by the Department of Real Estate Registration. The committee will conduct a site visit and request that the parties submit evidence and documents relevant to determining the property's value. After considering the information submitted and any information that the inspection committee was able to ascertain independently, the committee will determine the compensation that must be paid. The committee chairman will then inform the two parties and the Department of Real Estate Registration of its decision.

Both parties have the right to object to the value by notifying the chairman of the objection within ten days of the decision. If no objection is filed, the decision is final and binding. If one of the parties' objects to the decision of the inspection committee during the ten days, an appeal committee is formed. The appeal committee will review the information and documents submitted and announce the property's independent value. If the landowner is not satisfied with the value, he can inform the chairman of the appeal committee. The chairman will then notify the Department of Real Estate that the consensual acquisition has been revoked. In order to continue with the acquisition, the purchasing entity must, within sixty days, deposit the full compensation, as determined by the appeal committee, with the Department of Real Estate Registration. The acquisition then shifts from a consensual acquisition to a judicial acquisition.

PROCEDURES FOR JUDICIAL ACQUISITION

If the landowner and the acquiring entity cannot reach a consensual acquisition, then the property must be acquired by expropriation or eminent domain. Initially, the process is the same as a consensual acquisition. The acquiring entity requests the Department of Real Estate Registration to appoint an inspection committee to provide a value for the property. The landowner then has an opportunity to appeal, whence the appeals committee makes a decision.

In a judicial acquisition, the acquiring entity takes the final report of the appeals committee and files it with the court in the first instance. This report of value must be accompanied by a copy of the current record of the property, a map certified by the Department of Real Estate Registration specifying the footprint required for the public project, and a statement identifying the names of the owners of the property. Once the court has received all of the necessary information from the acquiring entity, the court schedules a date to consider the case. The court must consider three issues:

• Is the purpose for which the government takes the property a legitimate public interest?

• Is the subject property reasonably necessary for the project for which it is being acquired?

• Is the compensation that is being offered fair and just?

By law, once the acquiring entity has filed all the required documents with the court, the court must hold a hearing within ten days. Also, the court notifies the Department of Real Estate Registration to refrain from allowing further transactions concerning the property. The court then notifies the landowners of the initial hearing date. At the initial hearing, the court decides whether the purpose for which the government is taking the property serves a legitimate public interest and if the subject property is reasonably necessary for the purpose or project for which it is being acquired. If the court rejects either of these, it will deny the acquisition. However, suppose the court accepts that the property is being acquired for a legitimate public purpose and is reasonably necessary for the project. In that case, the court sets a trial date to hear evidence as to the value of the property. Following the trial, the court shall rule on its opinion of value. Either the acquiring entity or the landowner can appeal the court's decision of the first instance to the appeals court. The appeals court's decision can be appealed to the court of cassation. A decision by the court of cassation cannot be appealed. There is no appeal to the Supreme Court on land values.

PROCEDURES FOR ADMINISTRATIVE ACQUISITION

The procedures for administrative acquisition are nearly all within the central government and primarily within the prime minister's office. For example, if a province or city owns or controls property and an entity of the central government (ministry) needs that property for a public project, the ministry requests the prime minister's office. The prime minister's office has the authority to transfer control of the property to the ministry. The prime minister's authority extends to all government-owned lands (provincial, city, and national). Currently, 96% of all land in Zefuk is owned by the government.

TEMPORARY LAND USE (TEMPORARY SEIZURE)

In Zefuk, the government occupation of land for a period of less than two years is considered a temporary taking or temporary seizure. As with a permanent taking of property, a temporary seizure must be compensated. If the temporary seizure of property extends for a period over two years, the landowner can assert permanent (fee) takings.

The procedures for compensating for a temporary taking are significantly different from those for a permanent taking. Initially, there are similarities in that the government entity that needs to use the property may try to negotiate directly with the landowner. However, the compensation offered by the government entity needs to be supported by an opinion of value from the Department of Real Estate Registration. Suppose the government and the landowner cannot reach an agreement, or the government begins using the property without the landowner's agreement. In that case, the onus is upon the landowner to seek compensation.

In the case of a temporary taking, a landowner must file a request for compensation with the court of the first instance.

Unlike permanent takings, which are supported by opinions of value from the Department of Real Estate

154

Registration, the court does not have such evidence to determine value in temporary takings. In these cases, the court appoints a special master, typically a lawyer or retired judge, to ascertain the rental value of the temporarily seized property. The compensation is then determined by comparing the rental value of similar properties. In the case of Zefuk, the government is obligated to pay the landowner on a monthly basis for as long as the occupation persists. It's important to note that the landowner has the right to assert a permanent (fee) taking if the temporary seizure extends beyond two years.

LEASE CONTRACTS ACCORDING TO LEGISLATION

Understanding the legal framework is key to navigating the agricultural land in the Dokemy region. Most of this land is government-owned, either by the Ministry of Agriculture or the Department of Real Estate Registration. The majority of farmers have land lease contracts, but it's important to note that there are two distinct types: lease contracts regulated by Law 19 of 1980 and lease contracts regulated by the Land Reform Law of 1969. Each type has its own set of regulations and implications.

Under Law, lease contracts can be canceled without compensation. The second type of contract (under the Land Reform Law) requires the beneficiary ministry (e.g., the Ministry of Natural Resources) to pay compensation to the lessee. A committee involving the Agriculture Directorate, the Real Estate Department, Atukaz State Oil Company, and the Real Estate Registration decides the amount of compensation.

By law, Atukaz State Oil Company is the organization responsible for dealing with land issues related to oil investment in the Dokemy region. It's important to note that this responsibility falls on Atukaz State Oil Company, not the

155

International Oil Companies (IOS). This distinction is crucial for understanding the process and procedures involved in land lease contracts and compensation regulations.

When Atukaz State Oil Company requires a specific land site, Atukaz State Oil Company informs the Ministry of Agriculture or the State Real Estate Department about the acquisition of the land. The Ministry of Agriculture or the State Real Estate Department then cancels the lease contract with the farmers. The contracts of the first type can be canceled without payment of compensation. Some farmers have tried to go to court but could not receive compensation because the content of the lease states that the lessee will not be compensated if the government decides to re-acquire the land back from the lessee.

The second type of contract, regulated by the Land Reform, requires the beneficiary ministry to pay compensation to the lessee. The amount of compensation is decided by a committee involving the Agriculture Directorate, the Real Estate Department, Atukaz State Oil Company, and the Real Estate Registration. In most cases, the amount of compensation is low because the farmer is only compensated for the value of any construction(s) built on the land or the value of the crop, not the land itself. This process of compensation determination is important for the farmers to understand their rights and the factors that influence their compensation.

Some farmers have land deeds, which are treated as special cases under the law. In these cases, Atukaz State Oil Company would usually initiate a process of land confiscation and require the farmers to go to court. The court will then form a committee to evaluate the land, and Atukaz State Oil Company must pay the landowner the agreed compensation. This process of land confiscation and compensation determination is crucial for the farmers to understand their rights and the legal procedures they may face.

In the District of Dokemy, all these types of contracts (lease contracts under Land Reform Law of 1969, and land ownership deeds) are present. This diversity of contracts reflects the different circumstances and legal frameworks under which the land is leased or owned. Understanding this context is crucial for the farmers to know their rights and responsibilities under their specific type of contract.

LAWS AND REGULATIONS ASSOCIATED TO RESETTLEMENT

1. **Constitution of Zefuk - 2013** Prohibits the taking of private property without a fair compensation

2. **Acquisition Law - 1988**
   Authorized three types of government acquisition of property:
   Consensual Acquisition;
   Judicial Acquisition and Administrative Acquisition.
   Mandates the procedures for each type of acquisition.
   The law also sets temporary takings

3. **CPA Regulation - 2018**
   Commission for Resolution of Real Property Disputes collects and resolves Zefuk real property claims

4. **Real Estate Value Assessment Law - 1976**
   Authorized a tax on rents generated by real property.
   Resolution sets the rate of the tax

5. **Real Estate Rent Tax Law - 1955**
   Amended by CPA Order of 2004
   Authorized a tax on rents generated by real property

6. **Vacant Land Tax - 1959**
   Assesses an annual tax of 2% on the property's estimated value

7. **Real Estate Profits Tax Law - 1966**
   Assesses a tax on the sale or transfer of property

8. **Ministry of Public Services Law - 1962**
   The municipalities became responsible for land zoning and basic design of cities

9. **Land Rights Reconciliation Law - 1928**
   Authorized the government to take Arenuk lands and convert them to Usenuk lands. Intended to reduce the amount of Arenuk lands in favour of Usenuk lands

10. **Usenuk Law - 1959**
    Changed the definition of Usenuk to be an inheritable interest in real property

11. **Real Estate Registration Law - 1973**
    Created the current land registration process and is considered the main evidence to prove ownership and other rights

12. **Environmental Protection Law - 2007**

Mandates the inclusion of any resettlement as part of a comprehensive Environmental Impact Assessment (EIA). Provides penalties for noncompliance

13. Regulation of Water Well Drilling - 2001
Changes in water usage resulting from resettlement must be included in the
EIA and the project plan.
The Regulation of 2001 mandates the specifics of water well drilling

14. Water Law – 1999

15. Antiquities Law - 1932
The construction proponents must investigate, explore and excavate relics in coordination with the Heritage Committee of Zefuk

Chapter 4

LAND COMPENSATION AND RESETTLEMENT

EXECUTIVE SUMMARY

Scope and Approach

RECUSTAT is planning the development of Upper Banop, one of Zefuk's largest oil fields. The field is expected to produce 200,000 barrels per day by the end of 2034 and 2.05 million barrels per day over 15 years.

Seismic testing in Upper Banop is scheduled for April 2031. Workers involved in building the project infrastructure will have a base camp. By late 2030, approximately 50 workers are expected to be on-site, with up to 4,000 RECUSTAT employees and 12,000 personnel in total at peak construction.

RECUSTAT has entrusted its dedicated CSR Team with the crucial task of creating a Resettlement Action Plan Framework. This comprehensive plan addresses all matters relating to land access, compensation, and resettlement from the Upper Banop contract area, ensuring a fair and just process for all stakeholders involved.

In-country research conducted by the CSR Team of RECUSTAT ascertained that the Upper Banop contract area is inhabited, particularly along the Bigony River, which runs North to South through the western part of the contract area. Local residents also use the area for agricultural purposes, including cropping and raising livestock.

While land in the contract area is generally owned by the Ministry of Natural Resources, Ministry of Agriculture, and Ministry of Fisheries, a small portion is owned privately. The area is also home to internally displaced persons, who are protected by international law, whether or not they are landowners. As a consequence, a number of World Bank Operational Directives and International Finance Corporation performance standards relating to the resettlement of persons apply to Upper Banop.

Key Social Risks

The CSR Team's memorandum, titled Social Risk Management, has identified potential conflicts within and with the communities. However, RECUSTAT is not just aware of these risks, but is also taking proactive steps to mitigate them. This includes the preparation of a compensation or resettlement framework and extensive consultation with the local community.

Even though the contractor will conduct the seismic study and Atukaz State Oil Company is responsible for land acquisition, compensation, and resettlement, if conflict results, the reputation impact on RECUSTAT, as the first developer to commence seismic activities under this new oil field development regime, and on other international oil companies operating in southern Zefuk will be high.

The Resettlement Action Plan Framework

The Resettlement Action Plan Framework has been designed:

• To assist in building capacity among RECUSTAT and Atukaz State Oil Company staff by outlining the key concepts, principles, and legal requirements associated with the involuntary resettlement of stakeholders currently residing on and/or obtaining a livelihood from the Upper Banop contract area.

• To provide a series of steps that will enable RECUSTAT, Atukaz State Oil Company, and the project's contractors to implement minimum land access, compensation, and resettlement requirements within applicable legal requirements and international guidelines and the project's stringent schedule.

• To play a pivotal role in enabling RECUSTAT, in collaboration with Atukaz State Oil Company, to strategize, design, and execute a comprehensive Resettlement Action Plan

163

that adheres to international standards, thereby significantly reducing the potential for future conflict and mitigating the risk of negative reputation impacts on RECUSTAT.

• To provide recommendations for ongoing monitoring and evaluation of the Upper Banop resettlement process and throughout the project's life.

Conclusion

Effective resettlement planning requires:

1. Early consultation helps manage public expectations concerning a project's impact and expected benefits. Subsequent consultations provide opportunities for RECUSTAT and representatives of people affected by the project to negotiate compensation packages and eligibility requirements, resettlement assistance, and the timing of resettlement activities.

2. Process/transparency: Due to its inherent complexity, the resettlement of individuals, families, and enterprises will almost always give rise to grievances among the affected population.

3. Planning/implementation: Without preliminary and ongoing consultation with the local community and the development of a complete and proper Resettlement Action Plan, the potential for present and future conflict to arise between RECUSTAT, local residents, and within local communities is high.

INTRODUCTION

Project Background

Upper Banop is one of Zefuk's largest oil fields and is believed to hold 30 billion barrels of recoverable reserves, making it one of the largest fields in the world. The field is located in southern Zefuk, 98 miles South of Sadbokan, a major seaport. Most of the project area is agricultural land used for cropping and raising livestock. The area to the west has rainforests with hills and low mountains. The area to the southwest was previously wetland and marshland but has been drained and used for agricultural purposes. Most of the local population lives south of the project area, adjacent to the Bigony River. The Fadosa River runs to the northeast. The area may contain landmines, unexploded ordnance (UXO), and explosive remnants of war (ERW).

In 2030, RECUSTAT Oil Company was awarded the rights to develop the Upper Banop oil field. RECUSTAT will work to raise output from Upper Banop to 200,000 barrels per day by the end of 2034 and 2.05 million barrels per day over 15 years.

The Upper Banop oil field Development Contract is a partnership between Zefuk's Atukaz State Oil Company and the contracting Operator, RECUSTAT Oil Company. This agreement, set to last 25 years, includes a potential five-year extension. As per preliminary estimates, RECUSTAT's investments in the Upper Banop field are projected to reach approximately USD 500 million in 2030 and USD 6 billion over the following four to five years.

The Upper Banop field was discovered in 1988. Between 1989 and 1991, 21 wells were installed. New drilling operations at the Upper Banop field will start in 2032, with production beginning before the end of 2034. The target production level of over 750 million barrels of oil per year is expected to be reached in 2037. Development of the field will involve additional seismic work and drilling of more than four hundred wells.

There will be a base camp for workers involved in building the project infrastructure. By late 2030, approximately 50 workers are expected to be on-site, and the number will increase as construction progresses. At peak construction, up to 4,000 RECUSTAT employees and up to 12,000 personnel (including contractors) will be involved.

The extracted oil will be piped from the wells to the processing facility. Central processing facilities will be constructed to process up to 2.05 million barrels of oil per day. They will include 29 tanks and facilities for the treatment and reinjection of produced water. Initially, excess gas will be flared. As the project progresses, gas will be captured for use in power generation, and only a safety flare will remain.

In summary, the project will comprise:

• Wells and well pads.

• Central processing facility with flaring facility.

• Power station, possibly comprising gas turbines, run on gas from the wells.

• Export pipeline.

• Roads.

166

• Water supply infrastructure (river water intake, groundwater wells, desalination plant, and pipework).

• Camp(s).

2.2 Key Issues and Risks for Resettlement

Land Ownership, Resettlement and Compensation

Previous interviews and field observations conducted by the CSR Team have underscored the vital role of the Upper Banop contract area, particularly along the Bigony River, in agriculture. The area's exceptional fertility, a product of sedimentation from the river, sustains crucial agricultural activities such as cropping and livestock raising, making it a significant part of the local community's livelihood.

Initial investigations indicate that all land in the contract area is owned by three Ministries (Agriculture, Oil, and Finance). While there are believed to be internally displaced persons (IDPs) in the area, it's important to note that they are not considered landowners. However, as a group, IDPs are protected by international law, and any mistreatment is likely to draw significant international attention, underscoring the importance of adhering to international standards.

Under the terms of the contractual agreement between Atukaz State Oil Company and RECUSTAT, Atukaz is responsible for all matters relating to land access, compensation, and resettlement in the Upper Banop contract area. One of the critical issues for RECUSTAT concerning land acquisition, compensation, and resettlement is the intention and capacity of Atukaz State Oil Company to conduct project-related resettlement activities per international standards. It needs to be determined whether Atukaz State Oil Company has the capacity or the experience to design, forward-plan, and enact a resettlement program to international standards. RECUSTAT has requested that the CSR Team prepare a training plan for Atukaz State Oil Company staff in international land access, compensation, and resettlement guidelines. The training plan has been prepared, but the training has yet to be scheduled at this stage.

The implementation of international standards regarding the resettlement of persons from the Upper Banop project will contribute to the stability of the project's stakeholder environment. However, it's important to acknowledge that the implementation of global standards relating to the resettlement of persons will also assist in avoiding stakeholder outrage, which may result in potential delays and reputational impacts that may hinder the project's development schedule. As the development schedule currently stands, implementation of best practice standards within the provided timeframe will be challenging, particularly in light of the planned commencement of seismic activities as early as April 2031, before the commencement of stakeholder engagement or detailed resettlement action planning. We are fully aware of these potential risks and are prepared to address them with utmost caution and diligence.

Forthcoming Seismic Program

The CSR Team, with their extensive experience in managing social and environmental impacts, suggests that the Upper Banop oil field Operator use the best international practice and compensate internally displaced persons for their losses in the total replacement cost before the actual relocation. Displaced people will actively participate in relocation planning and should get reasonable support from the Operator's people while moving to another place. It is imperative to RECUSTAT as seismic activity is expected to be conducted across the

168

contract area starting in April 2031. The seismic survey process involves drilling shot holes into which small explosions are discharged to create seismic waves that reflect off oil reservoirs, indicating their position and size. The process requires traversing drilling and recording equipment across the seismic grid. In the case of the Upper Banop development, seismic activity may impact residences and fixed assets, gardens, cropping, and livestock activities in the contract area, potentially affecting access to gardens, agricultural activity, and mobility across the contract area. It may result in nuisance, noise, and disruption of residents and nearby communities. RECUSTAT should consider the resettlement before the seismic activity begins.

It is of utmost importance to note that without implementing a resettlement framework and before any consultation with the local community or developing a Resettlement Action Plan (RAP), the potential for conflict with and within the affected communities is significant. If it arises, this potential conflict could have a severe reputational impact on RECUSTAT, as the first project proponent to commence seismic activities under this new oil field development regime, and on other international oil companies operating in southern Zefuk.

The Early Activities Procedure aims to assist RECUSTAT, Atukaz State Oil Company, and the seismic program contractor in managing risk and implementing, at the least, minimum resettlement requirements in order to protect the project and its stakeholders.

Stakeholder Engagement

Linked to the risks outlined above is the matter of stakeholder engagement by RECUSTAT and its stakeholders in the Upper Banop area. At present, no stakeholder engagement has occurred: RECUSTAT is anonymous and has no presence in the area. To develop productive and positive relationships with the local community, consultation needs to happen as soon as possible, before the commencement of the seismic survey, and as an ongoing risk management strategy for the project.

The Stakeholder Study developed by the CSR Team identifies and profiles the project's key stakeholders and includes a detailed stakeholder engagement plan for the project's life. When used in conjunction with this resettlement framework, the stakeholder engagement plan will help facilitate effective stakeholder engagement and community consultation regarding the resettlement of affected persons and other project-wide issues.

One key issue that RECUSTAT still needs to clarify is the stakeholder engagement responsibilities between RECUSTAT and Atukaz State Oil Company to ensure consistency of messages and effective expectation management of stakeholders to avoid confusion and conflict.

Purpose of the Resettlement Framework

The purpose of the Resettlement Framework is fourfold.

First, the framework aims to assist in building capacity among RECUSTAT and the staff of Atukaz State Oil Company by outlining the key concepts, principles, and legal requirements associated with the involuntary resettlement of stakeholders currently residing on and/or obtaining a livelihood from the Upper Banop contract area.

Second, the framework seeks to provide a series of precise steps to enable RECUSTAT, Atukaz State Oil Company, and/or the project's contractors to implement minimum land access, compensation, and resettlement requirements, mindful of the applicable legal requirements and international guidelines. The recommendations section of this framework and the Early Activities Procedure, in particular, provide the minimum standards that should be adopted immediately by RECUSTAT in light of the project's tight and challenging project schedule.

Third, the framework seeks to provide a series of straightforward steps that, in the longer term, will enable RECUSTAT, in conjunction with Atukaz State Oil Company, to plan, design, and implement a Resettlement Action Plan (RAP) that will meet international standards. Such longer-term planning for a RAP will provide an opportunity to create a smooth and timely resettlement process that protects affected persons, minimizes the potential for conflict, and reduces the risk of damaging reputation impacts for RECUSTAT.

Fourth, the framework provides recommendations to enable the ongoing monitoring and evaluation of the Upper Banop Oil Field resettlement process and outlines the necessary steps required by the project's key partners throughout the project's life.

Objectives for the Resettlement Framework

It is important to emphasize that the Resettlement Framework outlines only the necessary issues, steps, and requirements to plan and implement a RAP and its associated consultation, engagement, and negotiation processes and provides a procedure for RECUSTAT, Atukaz State Oil Company, and its contractors that can be followed before the development of a complete and proper RAP, to at least fulfill some of the requirements. Consequently, the framework needs to constitute a complete and appropriate RAP to conduct physical resettlement of affected persons. To meet international standards, it must be supplemented by a full and proper RAP, which (as stated below) can be developed only following the conclusion of a series of stakeholder surveys, consultations, and detailed planning processes.

In light of the above limitations, the key objectives of the Resettlement Framework are:

• To ensure RECUSTAT and its project partners clearly understand the relevant legal requirements, international standards, and best practices for the resettlement of persons affected by the development of the Upper Banop Oil Field.

• Where resettlement cannot be avoided, outline the concepts and procedures for compensating persons affected by resettlement.

• To provide a framework for engaging and consulting affected persons and incorporating their key concerns and desires into the preparation of the RAP, wherever feasible.

• To summarize the key components of an internationally acceptable RAP and outline the process for developing and implementing such a plan.

• To summarize the key organizational issues that will require consideration and/or input from RECUSTAT and its project partners.

• To provide a framework for developing stakeholder feedback mechanisms and a monitoring and evaluation program for resettlement activities.

To provide a high-level procedure and associated responsibilities for immediate implementation regarding early project activities.

172

STANDARDS FOR

INVOLUNTARY RESETTLEMENT

Definitions of Involuntary Resettlement

According to the International Finance Corporation (IFC), resettlement of individuals from their land is considered involuntary when it occurs without the informed consent of the displaced persons or, if they give their consent, it is provided without having the power to refuse if they wished to do so (IFC, 2002). A typical example of involuntary resettlement is a government agency's land expropriation for a capital development project, as is the case with the Upper Banop Project.

Displacement as the result of a resource development project can be either physical or economic. Physical displacement is the actual physical relocation of people, resulting in a loss of shelter, productive assets, or access to productive assets (such as land, water, and forests). Economic displacement results from an action that interrupts or eliminates people's access to productive assets without physically relocating the people themselves. Consequently, while land acquisition does not necessarily require the displacement of people occupying or using the land, it may affect the living standards of people who depend on resources located in, on, or around that land (IFC, 2002). The IFC's resettlement policy is considered applicable in either situation.

International Standards and Best Practice

Many international oil companies operating in developing countries or rebuilding after years of conflict (reconstruction countries) find themselves in operating environments with limited laws and standards. Despite operating in an environment with a lack of national laws and regulations, these companies often face scrutiny from international civil society for failing to maintain social and environmental values. Due to the lack of legislation and regulation in social and environmental performance, many reputable companies operating in developing or reconstruction countries have adopted or developed internal guidelines and practices to maintain rigorous international health, safety, environmental, economic, and social performance. Project funding agencies such as the World Bank and the International Finance Corporation (IFC) have developed, through their experience, a set of guidelines and principles that presently exist as best practices for managing involuntary resettlement associated with resource development projects in developing countries.

Many in the international community consider the World Bank guidelines and the IFC's performance standards to be the most rigorous and appropriate guidelines for involuntary resettlement. These leading standards and guidelines also contribute to the social performance requirements of project development in developing and reconstruction countries. The following section presents these institutions' performance standards and guidelines.

Even where the project proponent is not seeking project financing from international financial institutions or export credit agencies, applying international standards and guidelines provides a robust framework for considering and implementing a RAP and its associated processes.

174

World Bank Operational Policy 4.12 – Involuntary Resettlement

The World Bank Operational Policy (OP) 4.12 on Involuntary Resettlement (World Bank, 2001) is accepted as the eminent guiding document, providing a good practice benchmark for involuntary resettlement projects. It describes the World Bank's policy and procedures on resettlement and also sets out the conditions that are expected to be met in projects involving community displacement.

The World Bank OP acknowledges that "involuntary resettlement may cause severe long-term hardship, impoverishment, and environmental damage unless appropriate measures are carefully planned and carried out" (World Bank, 2001). In order to minimize the likelihood or severity of such hardship, the OP recommends that the following principles and objectives be applied in all projects involving resettlement:

(a) Involuntary resettlement should be avoided where feasible or minimized, exploring all viable alternative project designs.

(b) Where it is not feasible to avoid resettlement, resettlement activities should be conceived and executed as sustainable development programs, providing sufficient investment resources to enable the persons displaced by the project to share in project benefits.

(c) Displaced persons should be meaningfully consulted and have opportunities to participate in planning and implementing resettlement programs.

(d) Displaced persons should be assisted in their efforts to improve their livelihoods and living standards or at least to restore them, in real terms, to pre-displacement levels or to levels

175

prevailing before the beginning of project implementation, whichever is higher.

The World Bank OP is supported by the IFC Performance Standard 5 – Land Acquisition and Involuntary Resettlement (IFC 2006,2012).

IFC Performance Standard 5 – Land Acquisition and Involuntary Resettlement

The following section specifies the IFC guideline for involuntary resettlement applicable to the Upper Banop Oil Field Project. The guideline and standard address both physical and economic resettlement based on damage to and/or deprivation of land, assets, income, and livelihoods. This information should be considered in the development of any Upper Banop Oil Field land acquisition and resettlement program.

The performance standard states that any resettlement activity requires consultation with disclosure of information to and active participation of the affected communities. The standards for such consultation are established during the environmental, social, and health assessment process and should be implemented by the client's social performance management team. As Atukaz State Oil Company will be implementing the resettlement activity, it is essential for RECUSTAT to ensure that Atukaz State Oil Company staff have the capacity to enact an RAP or any resettlement activities effectively. The standard applies to:

• Type I: Land rights for a private sector project acquired through expropriation or other compulsory procedures.

• Type II: Land rights for a private sector project acquired through negotiated settlements with property owners or those with legal rights to land, including customary or traditional

176

rights recognized or recognizable under the laws of the country if expropriation or other compulsory process would have resulted upon the failure of negotiation.

The key objectives of the performance standard include:

• To avoid or minimize involuntary resettlement wherever feasible by exploring alternative project designs.

• To mitigate adverse social and economic impacts from land acquisition or restrictions on affected persons' use of land by providing compensation for loss of assets at replacement cost and ensuring that resettlement activities are implemented with appropriate disclosure of information, consultation, and the informed participation of those affected.

• To improve or at least restore displaced persons' livelihoods and living standards.

• To improve living conditions among displaced persons by providing adequate housing with security of tenure at resettlement sites.

The standard requires the following considerations and applications of resettlement throughout the provided development phase:

• Project Design - Consideration of alternative project designs to avoid or at least minimize physical or economic displacement while balancing environmental, social, and financial costs and benefits.

• Compensation and Benefits for Displaced Persons - When displacement cannot be avoided, the project proponent will offer displaced persons and communities compensation for loss of assets at total replacement cost and other assistance to help them improve or at least restore their standards of living or livelihoods, as provided in this Performance Standard. Where livelihoods of displaced persons are land-based or collectively owned, the client will offer land-based compensation, where feasible. The project proponent will provide opportunities for displaced persons and communities to derive appropriate development benefits from the project.

• Consultation - Following disclosure of all relevant information, the project proponent will consult with and facilitate the informed participation of affected persons and communities, including host communities, in decision-making processes related to resettlement. Consultation will continue during the implementation, monitoring, and evaluation of compensation payment and resettlement to achieve outcomes consistent with this Performance Standard's objectives.

• Grievance Mechanism - The project proponent will establish a grievance mechanism consistent with Performance Standard 1 (Social and Environmental Assessment and Management System) to receive and address specific concerns about compensation and relocation raised by displaced persons or members of host communities. This mechanism will include a recourse mechanism designed to resolve disputes impartially.

• Resettlement Planning and Implementation - Where involuntary resettlement is unavoidable, the project proponent will carry out a census with appropriate socio-economic baseline data to identify the persons who will be displaced by the project, to determine who will be eligible for compensation and assistance, and to discourage the inflow of people who are ineligible for these benefits. Without host government procedures, the client will establish a cut-off date for eligibility. Information regarding the cut-off date will be well documented and disseminated throughout the project area. Standards for compensation will be transparent and consistent within the project.

Both the World Bank OP and IFC Performance Standard are further supported by the IFC Handbook for Preparing a Resettlement Action Plan (RAP) (IFC, 2002), which outlines the preparation of a RAP to ensure adherence to the standards within the operational policies and standards. The RAP signifies a commitment to meeting the obligations that arise from involuntary resettlement requirements. The recommendations are included in the IFC Handbook and thus are not discussed in detail here.

According to the World Bank and the IFC, resettlement activities are expected to be consistent with international standards even when host governments take responsibility for resettling affected people. This is the case with the Upper Banop Oil Field because Atukaz State Oil Company is responsible for land acquisition, compensation, and resettlement activities under the contract to develop the field.

Preparing a comprehensive and detailed RAP will enable RECUSTAT and its project partners to plan, implement, and monitor the resettlement process effectively. The process will include compensation payments, relocation initiatives, and any other related activities. In preparing a RAP, or at least considering the principles and guidelines of the performance standard and operational policy, RECUSTAT will place itself in a more strategic position to withstand local and international public scrutiny.

Oil and Gas Industry Best Practice

While not legally binding, the World Bank OP/IFC performance standards hold significant weight in the oil and gas industry. Numerous international companies, including some in

179

our sector, have publicly recognized these standards as the benchmark for resettlement activities, aligning with global best practice expectations (World Bank CSR Practice, 2004). Additionally, various industry bodies have developed their own guidance documents, all of which are rooted in the World Bank OP/IFC performance standards.

Existing RECUSTAT Social Codes and Public Commitments

According to information obtained from RECUSTAT, the Company has made a series of public statements and commitments with regard to social responsibility and participation in society, which are contained within the Social Code of RECUSTAT. The following section outlines the relevant commitments from the Social Code that, in conjunction with the recommendations outlined in this framework, provide the basis for the Company's approach to the processes required as part of the resettlement program for the Upper Banop project.

The Social Code is divided into three sections that address the following key issues:

1. Corporate social guarantees to the employees and non-working pensioners of RECUSTAT Oil Company.

2. Socially responsible participation in society.

3. Economic basis of social initiatives.

Of particular interest to this resettlement framework are the commitments contained within the Social Code states, while recognizing the new social obligations of business in conditions of growing inequality in access to worthwhile employment and benefits, the Company voluntarily commits itself to socially responsible participation in the life of the local population in the regions where RECUSTAT Group organizations operate and in society as a whole.

Using the Company's commitment as an overarching goal, RECUSTAT's approach to socially responsible participation in society includes but is not limited to:

(a) The Preservation of Distinctive National Cultures

(b) Promotion of Social Groups and Public Associations in Need of Support

(c) Charity Activities of the Company and Its Employees

(d) Participation in Social/Economic Development Programs Stipulated by Municipal, Regional and Federal Budgets

(e) Social Aspects of Business Reputation.

(f) Socially Responsible Relations with Contractors and Suppliers.

While the Social Code of RECUSTAT outlines our approach to socially responsible engagement with various stakeholders, it does not explicitly address resettlement activities. In light of this, leveraging their expertise, the CSR Team recommends that the specific requirements and procedures of the World Bank and IFC policies and standards reinforce the principles outlined in the Social Code. This alignment ensures our approach aligns with global norms and best practices.

RESETTLEMENT ACTION PLAN GUIDELINES

The information and steps detailed in the following section are based on the internationally recognized best practice approach to involuntary resettlement contained within the IFC Handbook for Preparing a Resettlement Action Plan (2002).

The IFC Handbook defines a RAP as a document drafted by the project proponent or other parties responsible for resettlement (such as government agencies, in this case, Atukaz State Oil Company) that specifies the procedures that the project proponent will follow and the actions it will take to resettle and compensate affected people and communities properly. The RAP is the project proponent's commitment to IFC (where applicable) and to the affected stakeholders and communities that it will meet its obligations arising from involuntary resettlement. It is provided in addition to any pre-existing social policies and commitments provided by the Company, such as the Social Code for RECUSTAT Oil Company, as it is specific to the project and resettlement.

Key Components of a Resettlement Action Plan

As stipulated in the IFC Handbook, the following list specifies the essential components of a comprehensive and internationally acceptable RAP:

• Identification of project impacts and affected populations.

• A legal framework for land acquisition and compensation.

• A compensation framework.

• A description of resettlement assistance and restoration of livelihood activities.

• A detailed budget.

• An implementation schedule.

• A description of organizational responsibilities.

• A framework for public consultation, participation, and development planning.

• A description of provisions for redress of grievances.

• A framework for monitoring, evaluation, and reporting.

The following section details, in short, the basic steps required to complete the key RAP components outlined above.

Key Steps in the RAP Planning and Implementation Process

Identification of Project Impacts and Affected Populations

The first task in planning resettlement is to identify a project's adverse impacts and the populations that will be affected. The task usually requires the participation of qualified experts who have appropriate training and experience. Given that the ultimate goal of a RAP is to enable those displaced by a project to improve their standard of living, this process requires a detailed examination of social, environmental, and economic conditions beyond simple physical inventories. Throughout the resettlement process, it is essential to bear in mind that the host communities (the community/communities to which the affected individuals and families are relocated) may be adversely affected by new settlements and population changes and should, therefore, be identified in their own right as a category of persons affected by the project.

IFC (2002) best practice states that affected populations and resettlement impacts should be identified through the following series of steps:

1. Thematic maps that identify such features as population settlements, infrastructure, soil composition, natural vegetation areas, water resources, and land use patterns.

2. A census that enumerates the affected people and registers them according to location.

3. An inventory of lost and affected assets at the household, enterprise, and community level.

4. Socio-economic surveys and studies of all affected people (including seasonal, migrant, and host populations), as necessary.

5. Analysis of surveys and studies to establish compensation parameters, design appropriate income restoration and sustainable development initiatives, and identify baseline monitoring indicators.

6. Consultation with affected populations regarding mitigation of effects and development opportunities.

RECUSTAT has commissioned a baseline characterization of the social and environmental situation in and around the Upper Banop contract area. The baseline characterization will provide information about the affected populations and resettlement impacts. However, more detailed data collection and analysis will be required to complete the RAP.

Legal Framework for Land Acquisition and Compensation

IFC requirements state that all applicable national, regional, and local laws and customs must be identified, reviewed, and included in the RAP. In the absence of specific laws relating to resettlement, the World Bank OP 4.12 provides the framework by which the resettlement process should be carried out. Even when national or local laws exist, if the requirements are less than the requirements outlined in the World Bank OP, then international best practice requires that the higher of the two requirements are met. Zefuk's legislation for compensation to landholders is minimal, and international best practice prevails.

Compensation Framework

A fundamental component of all RAPs is a thorough and equitably determined compensation framework that outlines the methodology for calculating the compensation entitlements of each affected stakeholder. According to IFC best practice, a RAP compensation framework specifies all forms of asset ownership or use rights among the affected population and outlines the project's strategy for compensating the population for the partial or complete loss of those assets.

The compensation framework should include, at a minimum, a description of:

1. Any compensation guidelines established by the host government

2. In the absence of established guidelines, the methodology that the project proponent will use to value losses

3. The proposed types and levels of compensation to be paid

4. Compensation and assistance eligibility criteria

5. Details outlining how and when compensation will be paid.

In order to ensure the success of the compensation program, adequate and timely consultation must be undertaken with all key stakeholders to assess the adequacy and acceptability of the proposed compensation framework.

RECUSTAT and Atukaz State Oil Company are responsible for demonstrating the adequacy of all compensation rates in the final RAP document. Once acceptable compensation rates are established, the project team should ensure that these rates are applied consistently throughout the project's life or adjust the rates consistently if compensation payments are staggered over the project's life. As specific compensation procedures may not be currently or adequately addressed by Zefuki law, the project compensation team will also be responsible for establishing an acceptable method for delivering compensation (either cash payments or in-kind allocations, as in the case of land-for-land compensation).

One of the fundamental tenets of the World Bank's involuntary resettlement policy is that (wherever feasible and desired by the affected people) land-based resettlement options should be provided to displaced people whose livelihoods are based on the use of the land (such as farmers and herders). This enables people to continue, where appropriate, subsistence activities rather than be driven to cities where cash payments quickly dissipate. As a significant number of landholders are thought to grow crops, garden, and herd sheep in the Upper Banop contract area, it is important to plan for equivalent or superior land-based resettlement options.

In situations where cash compensation is deemed more appropriate (or where affected persons, after informed consultation, choose cash rather than land-for-land compensation), the IFC recommends that the project's compensation team should calculate and award compensation payments according to an array of compensation principles that retain and/or restore their standard of living.

Eligibility Criteria for Compensation

RECUSTAT and Atukaz State Oil Company are responsible for establishing and clearly disclosing the criteria by which affected people will be considered eligible for compensation and other resettlement assistance. The procedure should include provisions for consultations with affected persons, households, community leaders, local authorities, and as appropriate, non-government organizations.

Under the IFC policy, displaced persons with formal and no formal legal rights to land or other affected assets are entitled to compensation for loss of land or other assets, such as dwellings and crops taken for project purposes, and resettlement assistance.

RECUSTAT and Atukaz State Oil Company must know that under the IFC requirements, the absence of legal title to land or other assets is not a bar to compensation for lost assets or other resettlement assistance. Seasonal resource users, such as herders or fishing families, hunters, and gatherers, may have interdependent economic relations with communities located within the project area that will be adversely affected by resettlement. The existence of such populations and economic relationships can be determined through direct stakeholder consultation and socio-economic surveys.

Compensation Rates

It is impossible to effectively determine adequate compensation rates without a detailed analysis of the types of infrastructure, vegetation, trees, and other assets that may require compensation and comparing this information with localized market rates and prices. Table 10 indicates the types of assets found within the contract area that may require compensation. Still, a detailed study, including consultation and negotiation with affected persons, is expected to be conducted by RECUSTAT or Atukaz State Oil Company before finalizing a compensation agreement. Compensation rates should consider the replacement costs necessary to re-establish the same assets and infrastructure in a new location.

Table 10

Indicative table of assets found in the Upper Banop contract area

Asset	Example Compensation Basis
Residences	Size (per square feet); construction type (based on construction, roofing, flooring material); replacement cost (materials and labor).
Other physical assets: fences; external kitchen or toilet; animal shelter; shrine; grave.	Size (per square feet); construction type (based on construction, roofing, flooring material); replacement cost (materials and labor).
Business Dwellings (shop, stall, workshop, etc.)	Size (per square feet); construction type (based on construction, roofing, flooring material); replacement cost (materials and labor); earnings loss.
Productive Trees (for food production, construction material firewood)	Value of product; number of trees affected; future product loss.
Fuel Sources (firewood)	Value of product; quantity affected.
Crops (grain, vegetable)	Value of product; quantity affected; future product loss.
Vegetable Gardens	Size; value of product; quantity affected; future product loss.
Aesthetic Gardens (flowers, shrubs, etc.)	Size; replacement cost.

Naturally Occurring Vegetation	Value of product; quantity affected; future product loss.
Water Well	Replacement cost; cost of intermediary supply.
Livestock Pens/Dwellings	Replacement cost.

Social Equality

Women comprise a disproportionately large number of people with low incomes in Zefuk, with women's employment at only 17%. Culturally engrained gender discrimination tends to limit women's access to resources and as a result, women are often the first to suffer when resettlement is planned or poorly executed.

In order to comply with international best practices, RECUSTAT and Atukaz State Oil Company must ensure that eligibility criteria for relocation and cost recovery are balanced for women, whose incomes tend to be lower and less stable than men. Eligibility for relocation and the allocation of new sites should be made to the head of the household, regardless of whether they are male or female. Land titles, use-right agreements, or loan titles should be registered in the name of both husband and wife or the woman's name if she is the head of the household.

Some of the immediate and practical initiatives that can be considered to improve women's adaptation to the resettlement site include:

• Ensuring ownership and compensation entitlements are issued in the name of wife and husband.

190

• Improving health services by providing training for village midwives, primary health care centers, child spacing/family planning counseling, clean water supply, and sanitation training.

• Improving family services by providing immunizations, childcare for wage-earning women, primary schools, inputs for food-crop production, and housing.

• Increasing incomes by setting up credit groups, skills training, and market access.

Vulnerable groups can include households headed by women, households victimized by war and disease that children head, households made up of the aged or handicapped, households whose members are impoverished, or households whose members are socially stigmatized (as a result of traditional or cultural bias) and economically marginalized. Special assistance to vulnerable groups may consist of the following:

• Provision for separate and confidential consultation.

• Priority in site selection in the host area.

• Relocation near to kin and former neighbors.

• Provision of a contractor, if necessary, to construct their new house.

• Assistance with dismantling salvageable materials from their original home.

• Priority access to all other mitigation and development assistance.

• Monitoring nutritional and health status to ensure successful integration into the resettled community.

The RAP should document the rehabilitation measures the sponsor will implement for all vulnerable groups during the physical relocation and rehabilitation of affected communities.

Resettlement Assistance and Restoration of Livelihood Activities

The IFC recommends that project proponents undertake the following actions on behalf of all affected people, including members of the host communities in which displaced people will be settled:

• Inform affected people of their options and rights concerning resettlement.

• Provide technically and economically feasible options for resettlement based on consultation with affected people and assessment of resettlement alternatives.

• Whether physical relocation is required or not, provide affected people with prompt and adequate compensation at total replacement value for loss of assets due to project activities.

• Where physical relocation is necessary, provide assistance with relocation expenses (moving allowances, transportation, special assistance, and health care for vulnerable groups).

• Where physical relocation is necessary, provide temporary housing, permanent housing sites, and resources (in cash or in-kind) for the construction of permanent housing - inclusive of all fees, taxes, customary tributes, and utility hook-up charges.

• Provide affected people with transitional financial support (such as short-term employment, subsistence support, or salary maintenance).

• Where necessary, provide affected people with development assistance and compensation for lost assets described above, such as land preparation, agricultural inputs, credit facilities, and training and employment opportunities.

RECUSTAT and Atukaz State Oil Company must ensure that they undertake all land acquisition, provide compensation for lost assets, and initiate resettlement related to a specific project before any project activities commence. In particular, land and other assets should not be acquired until compensation is paid and, where applicable, resettlement sites and moving allowances are provided to displaced persons.

Given that RECUSTAT intends to begin conducting seismic studies in the contract area before any stakeholder consultation and resettlement planning, all steps must be outlined in the Early Activities Procedure. This framework's Early Activities Procedure is strictly adhered to and understood by all project contractors.

Although the Zefuki government (through Atukaz State Oil Company) has assumed responsibility for resettlement, international expectations will require RECUSTAT to use its influence with Atukaz State Oil Company to explain the best practice approaches and, if feasible, negotiate performance-based implementation agreements linking the disbursement of funds in installments to the achievement of agreed-upon milestones.

Physical resettlement of people affected by the project will require the following components:

- Site Selection and Preparation.

- Influx Management.

- Relocation Schedule and Assistance.

- Replacement of Services and Enterprises.

- Livelihood Restoration.

- Land-based livelihood.

- Wage-based livelihoods.

- Enterprise-based livelihoods.

- Treatment of Cultural Property.

- Special Assistance for Women and Vulnerable Groups.

Budget and Implementation Schedule

The RAP budget must justify all assumptions made when calculating compensation rates and other cost estimates, and both physical and cost contingencies must be considered. As previously noted, the cash value of compensation packages should be indexed to US dollars or another stable currency to protect those eligible for cash compensation from local currency devaluation or inflation.

In situations where the host government assumes responsibility for the payment of compensation and resettlement assistance allowances, as is the case with the Upper Banop project, the project proponent should collaborate with the

194

responsible government agency to ensure that payments are made on schedule. If the project proponent is financing government resettlement efforts, it should do so in installments and link the disbursement of funds to performance-based milestones.

The RAP budget should be linked with a detailed implementation schedule for all key resettlement and rehabilitation activities. This schedule should be synchronized with the project's civil works construction schedule. Timing of the RAP field activities, such as consultation, census, and survey implementation, is crucial. Commencing field activities too soon before the project begins may raise local expectations and attract newcomers. Alternatively, the commencement of activities too late after the project starts may interfere with project implementation and create anger amongst the relocating population. Planners should be attentive to the agricultural and employment cycles of affected people and avoid scheduling key resettlement activities at times that may disrupt these cycles. Linking resettlement and construction schedules ensures that project managers place key resettlement activities on the same critical path as key project construction activities. Linking schedules in this way creates an imperative for coordinating resettlement with other project activities throughout the chain of project management.

Organizational Responsibilities

The RAP must identify and provide details on the roles and responsibilities of all organizations (public, private, governmental, or non-governmental) responsible for resettlement activities. For Upper Banop, it is understood that Atukaz State Oil Company is responsible for the acquisition of land and payment of compensation. However, this process will require involvement and support by RECUSTAT or contracted third parties to ensure it is conducted to best practice standards.

Regardless of implementation responsibilities, the World Bank Resettlement Policy expects the project proponent to take responsibility for assessing the capacity of its resettlement partners to carry out their duties. Whilst host governments may reserve the right to manage land acquisition, compensation payments, and resettlement associated with a project, international best practice requires the outcome of an RAP to conform to the objectives of the World Bank involuntary resettlement policy.

Stakeholder Consultation

Depending on the scale of resettlement associated with the Upper Banop project, it may be appropriate to create a resettlement advisory group (or steering committee or task force) to coordinate the implementation of a RAP. The advisory group should comprise representatives of RECUSTAT and Atukaz State Oil Company, relevant government lines and administrative departments, community organizations, non-government organizations involved in resettlement, and representatives of the communities affected by the project, including host communities. The advisory group should convene at regular intervals during the design and implementation phases of the RAP to ensure the regular exchange of information among all parties and the coordination of all resettlement activities. Membership of the advisory group should include government representatives with the requisite authority over both line and administrative departments. This level of authority is required to ensure the timely implementation of resettlement activities and redress grievances.

Regardless of the extent to which it is directly responsible for the implementation of the RAP, it is expected that RECUSTAT will designate an individual within the project management structure to coordinate the construction and resettlement activities of the project. Preferably, this

196

individual's responsibilities should be dedicated to RAP implementation.

Public Consultation, Participation, and Development Planning

Effective resettlement planning requires regular consultation with a wide range of project stakeholders. Broadly defined, stakeholders include any individual or group affected by or believes it is affected by the project. They also include any individual or group that can play a significant role in shaping or influencing the project, either positively or negatively, including the host community.

A public hearing helps explain a project's impact and expected benefits to the public. Subsequent consultations provide opportunities for the sponsor and representatives of people affected by the project to negotiate compensation packages and eligibility requirements, resettlement assistance, and the timing of resettlement activities.

There are three key components of effective stakeholder consultation. The first is to ensure there is a free flow of information between project proponents and key stakeholders in order to assure the alignment of the project team and stakeholders and their agreement (wherever possible) about the objectives of the project and associated resettlement. As early as possible in the project development process, project partners should:

• Identify all stakeholders.

197

• Inform local government, village leaders, and local community organizations of the project plan as soon as feasible and ask them to inform their constituents.

• Brief all project line managers and personnel who will interact regularly with people affected by the project regarding the anticipated effects of the project and measures to mitigate its impact.

• After completing the census and the public notice of the eligibility cut-off date, arrange for the government to issue a formal notice banning the construction or approval of construction of new buildings or capital improvements in areas affected by the project.

• Prepare an illustrated resettlement information booklet providing details on eligibility, compensation rates, other entitlements, a timetable for implementation, and all applicable grievance procedures.

• Prepare and issue regular resettlement information updates.

Keeping affected people fully informed of their rights and responsibilities is crucial to the success of resettlement planning. To achieve this objective, information must be made accessible and understandable. Information should be translated into local dialects. It should also consider including media accessible to literate and non-literate individuals (such as radio, television, mobile video broadcasting, public notice boards, newspapers, leaflets and flyers, town representatives, and door-to-door canvassing). Once again, special efforts should be made to reach vulnerable groups lacking access to public media and information exchange.

The second key component is the effective promotion of stakeholder participation. IFC requirements state that project proponents must initiate and facilitate a series of consultations with project stakeholders throughout the planning and implementation of a RAP. These consultations aim to inform stakeholders about the project and its effects and provide opportunities for people to voice their concerns and propose alternatives. Formal consultations convened by RECUSTAT and its project partners should include RECUSTAT and Atukaz State Oil Company representatives, project managers, other relevant government authorities, representatives of concerned non-government organizations, and members of both displaced and host communities. The objective of these consultations should be to secure the participation of all people affected by the project in their resettlement planning and implementation. Regular consultation with affected people allows project management to monitor the adequacy and effectiveness of the RAP's compensation packages, livelihood restoration efforts, and development initiatives.

The third and final key component of effective stakeholder consultation is documenting all information disclosure and public consultation efforts. The documentation should identify who was consulted, what was discussed, and what follow-up was required.

Due to the complexities of the Upper Banop resettlement program and the limited timeframe for its implementation, it is recommended that RECUSTAT employ an in-house community liaison representative with a budget specifically for the facilitation and management of public consultation. As previously mentioned, the stakeholder study report provides further project-specific information regarding steps for stakeholder engagement and community consultation.

Redress of Grievances (Feedback Mechanisms)

Due to its inherent complexities, the resettlement of individuals, families, and enterprises will almost always give rise to grievances among the affected population over issues ranging from rates of compensation and eligibility criteria to the location of resettlement sites and the quality of services at those sites.

Timely redress of such grievances is vital to the satisfactory implementation of resettlement and completion of the project on schedule. Consequently, RECUSTAT should seek to ensure adequate procedures are in place to allow affected people to lodge a complaint, claim, or general feedback without cost to them and with the assurance of a timely and satisfactory response. Once again, special consideration may be required to ensure that women and members of vulnerable groups have equal access to grievance redress and general feedback procedures. This may include enabling, via capacity building and training, the women, or members of vulnerable groups to facilitate the grievance redress and feedback process or to ensure that groups representing the interests of women and other vulnerable groups take part in the process.

Grievances are best redressed through the project team, local civil administration, or other mediation channels acceptable to all parties. Such channels of mediation may involve customary and traditional institutions of dispute resolution. The project team should make every effort to resolve grievances at the community level. Recourse to the legal system should be avoided except as a last resort.

Under circumstances like the Upper Banop project, where Atukaz State Oil Company has assumed responsibility for resettlement, RECUSTAT may need help guaranteeing fair and timely grievance redress. Despite this reality, international best practice still requires RECUSTAT to ensure proper grievance redress procedures are in place and monitor those procedures to ensure that grievances are effectively addressed.

The RAP should describe the grievance redress framework that will be established by either Atukaz State Oil Company or RECUSTAT. The description should include:

• Institutional arrangements.

• Procedures for recording and processing grievances.

• Mechanisms for adjudicating grievances and appealing judgments.

• A schedule, with deadlines, for all steps in the grievance redress process.

In conjunction with the development of this resettlement framework, the CSR Team has also developed a detailed Stakeholder Engagement Plan as part of a broader Stakeholder Study conducted for the Upper Banop project. Further project-specific information regarding steps for stakeholder engagement and community consultation, including recommendations regarding minimum steps to be implemented before the commencement of the seismic study, can be obtained from the Stakeholder Study.

Monitoring, Evaluation, and Reporting

The objective of monitoring is to provide RECUSTAT with feedback on RAP implementation and to identify problems and successes as early as possible to allow timely adjustment of implementation arrangements. For these reasons, RAP monitoring and evaluation activities should be adequately funded, implemented by qualified specialists, and integrated into the overall project management process.

The RAP must provide a coherent monitoring plan that identifies the organizational responsibilities, the methodology, and the schedule for monitoring and reporting. The two critical components of a monitoring plan should be performance monitoring and impact monitoring. The scope of the monitoring plan should be commensurate with the scale and complexity of the RAP.

Performance Monitoring

Performance monitoring is an internal management function allowing RECUSTAT and Atukaz State Oil Company to measure physical progress against milestones established in the RAP. Performance milestones could include:

1. Public meetings held.

2. Census, assets inventories, assessments, and socioeconomic studies completed.

3. Grievance redress procedures in place and functioning.

4. Compensation payments disbursed.

5. Housing lots allocated.

6. Housing and related infrastructure completed.

7. Relocation of people completed.

8. Income restoration and development activities initiated.

9. Monitoring and evaluation reports submitted.

202

As noted above, the RAP's performance monitoring should be integrated into the overall project management to ensure that RAP activities are synchronized with all project implementation activities. Performance monitoring reports should be prepared at regular intervals (monthly, quarterly, semi-annually, and annually), beginning with the commencement of any resettlement-related activities.

Impact Monitoring

Impact monitoring gauges the effectiveness of the RAP and its implementation in meeting the needs of the affected population. Depending on the scale of resettlement, impact monitoring is conducted by the project's management or an independent external agency. The purpose of impact monitoring is to provide RECUSTAT with an up-to-date assessment of resettlement's effects, verify internal performance monitoring, and identify adjustments in the implementation of the RAP as required. Where feasible, affected people should be included in all phases of impact monitoring, including the identification and measurement of baseline indicators.

The effects of a RAP are tracked against the baseline conditions of the population that were identified during the census surveys and inventories conducted prior to resettlement. RECUSTAT or Atukaz State Oil Company will need to establish objectively verifiable indicators to measure the impact of physical relocation on the health, welfare, and livelihoods of the affected population and the effectiveness of impact mitigation measures.

The RAP should budget sufficient resources to finance independent monitoring of these indicators by qualified professionals on a regular basis during RAP implementation. The monitoring should continue for several years beyond the completion of the RAP to ensure that the project's income restoration efforts and development initiatives have succeeded and that the affected population has successfully re-established itself at its new site.

In addition to the quantitative indicators described above, impact monitoring should be supplemented by qualitative indicators to assess the satisfaction of affected people with resettlement initiatives and, thus, their adequacy. The most effective qualitative monitoring methodology is direct consultation with the affected populations through regular meetings, focus group discussions, or similar forums established by RECUSTAT for public participation as part of the consultation framework.

Project-wide principles for Upper Banop project resettlement

Based on the best practice standards and international expectations detailed in this framework, the CSR Team recommends that the following resettlement principles be adopted by the Upper Banop project team, including Atukaz State Oil Company and RECUSTAT representatives, before the commencement of any seismic studies and/or resettlement activities. Please refer to Table 11

Table 11

General Principles	
R1.	A resettlement project team (RPT), including RECUSTAT, Atukaz State Oil Company and relevant contractors, should be established to manage and monitor resettlement activities. Within this team, a specific contact person should be employed or nominated to oversee the community consultation process and manage incoming feedback and grievances

R2.	The RPT will develop a General Compensation Policy based on the best practice principles contained in this framework that will be adopted by the RECUSTAT at the highest level
R3.	Involuntary relocation of existing residences and associated structures will be avoided wherever possible, and this process of minimization will bear in mind the possibilities for future project expansion
R4.	Where resettlement is unavoidable, RECUSTAT will adhere, to the greatest extent possible, to the best practice international standards outlined in this resettlement framework
R5.	The RPT will establish clear responsibilities and timelines to be adhered to by all project partners (including Atukaz State Oil Company), contractors and employees
R6.	The RPT will define a clear and consistent schedule of costs, including compensation agreements, to ensure that all affected persons receive consistent compensation and treatment. This process also maintains transparency to avoid misapplication or dissatisfaction
Timing of Resettlement Activities	
R7.	Where relocation of settlements is necessary, it shall only occur after adequate consultation and negotiation with, and the agreement of, the affected persons
R8.	In the event of the planned seismic program, where time for adequate consultation does not exist, RECUSTAT will a) consider rescheduling its seismic program to allow for adequate consultation or b) at a minimum, avoid residences and be prepared to pay consistent and equitable compensation for damage to agriculture or other land use that contributes to livelihoods, at the time of disturbance
Stakeholder Engagement and Consultation	
R9.	Local government and tribal leaders should be present at all negotiations on relocation and resettlement in which they are impacted

R10.	Transparency in negotiations for relocation will be observed. Full written records of all meetings, discussions, and agreements (affirmed formally by all parties to such discussions) shall be kept and be publicly available
R11.	Special attention should be paid to ensure that vulnerable groups, such as women, youth, and disabled persons, are included in the stakeholder engagement process. This may require the facilitation of specific consultation session run only by women, held in particular location, or at particular times of the day
Land Allocation and Compensation	
R12.	Resettlement will, wherever possible, be to sites with ready access to affected stakeholders' land (where such land is not itself occupied by the project). If such existing settlements are located along roads, then relocation will be to sites with equally good access to commercial/transportation opportunities (if this is requested by the affected community)

R13.	The project will pay compensation for all assets lost as a result of relocation under the terms of the abovementioned General Compensation Policy, as well as ensuring that, among other matters, it:
	
	(a) bears all reasonable costs of physical relocation
	
	(b) provides materials for affected persons to build new housing
	
	(c) pays an allowance for the labor costs of such building
	
	(d) prepares (or pay all costs associated with the preparation)
	            relocation sites including UXO clearance
	
	(e) pays an allowance for loss of income incurred because of
	            relocation (if appropriate/required)

R14.	When identifying resettlement locations and host communities, the project team will pay special attention to ensuring that relocated persons have access to land and water than is uncontaminated
	Feedback Mechanisms
R15.	The RPT will develop, implement, and advertise feedback mechanisms, such as letter drop boxes, community notice boards, suggestion boxes, telephone hotlines and an email address, should be implemented and advertised to all affected peoples
R16.	The RPT will appoint a dedicated contact officer for issues associated with resettlement activities, who can be easily contacted by affected persons. The contact officer should reside in the communities or local area and work as a liaison between then RPT and the communities

Early Activities Procedure

Due to the tight development schedule for the Upper Banop project and the planned commencement of seismic testing activities before any community consultation and resettlement planning has taken place, it is recommended that all project personnel and contractors (including the contracted seismic study term) are appropriately inducted and familiarized with the steps outlined in the following Early Activities Procedure (EAP).

It must be noted that this procedure is designed to supplement the detailed recommendations outlined above and contained in the World Bank and IFC best practice policy and standards. Rather, it has been designed in recognition of the need to outline the absolute minimum requirements that must be implemented during all early project activities. The minimum requirements should be progressively built upon until all recommendations outlined in this framework, including developing a complete and proper RAP, are addressed.

Resettlement Project Team Responsibilities

Ensure a project team member has consulted the relevant local government authorities and tribal leaders to ensure they are aware of the activity, willing and able to provide information to community members and report data back to the project team.

Develop a standard pack of information, including a description of activities, what landowners/occupiers can expect in terms of impacts and potential damage, any potential safety hazards, or other issues they should be aware of, and information on how any necessary compensation will be calculated and paid.

Develop and implement a grievance mechanism for people aggrieved by the seismic process. This mechanism will likely involve providing contact details for a dedicated project person who will be responsible for addressing grievances and compensation claims within the project information pack.

Ensure an RECUSTAT community relations person from the project team accompanies all early project activities and acts as a liaison with affected community members.

RECUSTAT Personnel or Contractor Procedure

Step 1: Identification of Impact Area

• Identify areas to be impacted by specific activity and compare with available population data.

• Identify affected landowners and occupiers.

Step 2: Activity Design

• Wherever possible, design or amend the activity to avoid existing buildings, public infrastructure (toilets, storage areas, etc.), areas with livestock, crops, gardens, or productive vegetation, and environmentally or culturally sensitive areas.

Step 3: Landowner/Occupier Contact

• Inform landowners and occupiers in advance of the intention to access their land. Include information such as the date, approximate time, and expected duration of the seismic activity on their land.

• If advanced notice is not possible, ensure that these people are located and the information is provided on the first day of the study before activities commence.

• Provide landowners and occupiers with an information pack (mentioned above), confirm their understanding of the material, and provide the opportunity for questions.

• Ensure that landowners and occupiers understand the grievance mechanism and know how to contact the project team to provide feedback, complain, or seek information about compensation.

Step 4: Risk Assessment

• Conduct a daily onsite risk assessment to identify any previously unidentified safety hazards and potential for damage.

• Update landowners and occupiers as needed if risk assessment outcomes change.

Step 5: Record the State of Existing Buildings and Environment

• Seek permission to photograph and record details of any dwellings, infrastructure, or productive land within a 500-foot radius of the seismic activity.

• Where possible, record exact GPS coordinates of land disturbed by seismic activity.

• This information should be provided to the resettlement project team after the activities so that, if required, it can be utilized to determine the nature and validity of any reported damage as a result of early project activities, as well as assist in determining the amount of compensation to be paid if this has not been previously identified.

Step 6: Record Details of Any Damage Caused During the Study

• If it is determined that damage has occurred, the project personnel or contractor must compile a detailed inventory of damage caused. The inventory should include the area damaged;

the nature of the land use (type of crop, irrigated or rain-fed, livestock grazing, water source, etc.); the number and type of productive trees and shrubs damaged; the amount and type of wood sources damaged or destroyed; other immoveable physical assets damaged or destroyed (such as water wells, fences, graves, etc.); and any other information that will assist in determining the amount and type of compensation to be paid to the landholder/user.

• The inventory must then be lodged with a contact from the resettlement project team, who will accept responsibility for addressing the damage and paying compensation as required. Timely payment of compensation for damage will be critical to harmonious relations with affected persons, particularly where their ability to exist or earn an income is constrained.

RECUSTAT ORGANIZATIONAL REQUIREMENTS

Key Steps for an Upper Banop Resettlement Action Plan

The resettlement of communities from within the Upper Banop contract area in line with international best practices will require the implementation of the following initiatives:

1. Identification of Affected People and Assets

2. Detailed household survey and identification of any vulnerable groups

3. General agreement on items in the compensation package

4. Individual household interviews to cover individual concerns

5. Conducting a pre-implementation impact assessment

6. Planning the move

7. Implementing the move

8. Conducting a post-implementation monitoring and evaluating the outcomes of the process

To successfully achieve these outcomes, the Key Steps in the RAP Planning and Implementation Process will need to be considered, designed, implemented, and reviewed.

Table 12 aligns the necessary steps in the RAP Planning and Implementation Process with the key action steps, timeframes, and responsibilities for the Upper Banop project team as a checklist tool.

Table 12

Checklist tool - Key steps in the RAP planning and implementation process

RAP Stage	Action Steps
Impact and Affected Population Identification	• Commission census surveys, asset inventory and socio-economic studies of affected populations to determine resettlement numbers. Potential impacts and items requiring compensation

Legal Framework	• Conduct detailed examination of local and national legal framework for resettlement in Zefuk
Compensation Framework	• Develop a fair and equitable compensation framework based on abovementioned legal framework, World Bank and IFC principles and locally agreed market value of land, assets, and goods
Resettlement and Livelihoods Assistance	• Assess the extent to which the livelihoods and development opportunities of affected peoples are likely to be influenced by resettlement and develop and associated plan to assist resettled peoples to re-establish (and ideally improve) their livelihood capabilities
Budgeting	• Develop a detailed budget to cover all elements of the RAP and resettlement process, including necessary specialist studies, public consultation, and compensation
Implementation Schedule	• Align the RAP framework with the overall project schedule to development a master plan that allows adequate time for resettlement activities, including consultation and negotiation activities with affected peoples
Public Consultation	• Develop a detailed public consultation program that includes participation by all identified stakeholders (or their legitimate representatives) and create specific opportunities for participation by vulnerable groups

Grievance and Feedback Mechanisms	• Develop and implement a series of grievance and feedback mechanisms to allow for regular communication from the affected peoples and timely resolution of resettlement associated community issues
Monitoring, Evaluation and Reporting	• Develop a monitoring, evaluation, and reporting process to regularly check progress of the RAP against performance and impact monitoring criteria

Chapter 5

CONCLUSIONS
AND
RECOMMENDATIONS

SOCIAL COMMITTEE AS A MEDIATOR IN
CONFLICTS RESOLUTION

The morning sun never lasts a day. Every social project ends someday. Therefore, social projects must contribute to the community's sustainable development throughout its existence. Give a man a fish, and you feed him for a day; teach a man to fish, and you will feed him for a lifetime. This means social activity must strive to build independent capacity in communities, igniting a spark of empowerment that can fuel their own development. Projects should align with local development plans and, as far as possible, rely on the communities' own efforts.

It is not just important but essential for all social projects to have a well-defined exit strategy. This strategy not only avoids creating dependencies but also ensures the project's long-term sustainability and the community's independence. The urgency and importance of this aspect cannot be overstated, as it is a key factor in the success of any social project.

In the first chapter, I wrote about the Social Committee of the Project and its vital role in ensuring smooth oil operations and avoiding mass protests and work stoppages. The role of the Social Committee is to organize constructive interaction between the potentially conflicting parties and resolve their conflict. In fact, the Committee acts as a mediator in these relations within the local community and in relations between the Operator of oil development project and the local community.

The Social Committee, a pivotal entity, acts as a buffer or lightning rod and, ultimately, a crucial element of the exit strategy. It is the Social Committee that takes the first blow of people's anger and is the culprit of unfair decisions; they are responsible for the employment of the local population, determining the route of the mountain road along which the drilling fluid is brought to the drilling cluster at an altitude of 1000 miles. The Social Committee, comprised of local representatives, plays a significant role in empowering the local population by employing them at Contractors and Subcontractors firms of the Operator. The Social Committee decides who will receive benefits and who will not, thereby ensuring the project's success is in the hands of the community. This decision-making process is transparent and participatory, with the committee consulting with the community and

216

considering their needs and concerns before making any decisions.

Project proposals for social investments are not developed in isolation but in consultation with the local benefactors or target groups that the project is intended to benefit. The active involvement of project beneficiaries in project identification and implementation significantly enhances the project's sustainability, making their participation invaluable. Thanks to the presence of the Social Committee, RECUSTAT Oil Company is not a decision-maker for local people. That is why it is not responsible for the social project's content and its implementation's place. This approach ensures that the community's needs and aspirations are at the forefront of the project, leading to its success and the community's empowerment.

Considering the cultural and historical characteristics of the Upper Banop area and the tribes inhabiting it, a unique recruitment mechanism was developed. The adopted mechanism ensured a proportional selection of candidates from a particular tribe, depending on its size, land area, etc. This system maintained balance in inter-tribal relations and, therefore, stability in the Contract Territory. It's worth noting that this was mainly due to the Committee members' position of neutrality towards the tribes. The first Social Committee included nine tribal leaders and eight local authorities. Due to the regular conflicts and contradictions between tribes, Atukaz State Oil Company proposed a new composition of the Social Committee. According to the tribal sheikhs, it includes only - the Sheikh of Dara tribe, who lives directly in the Contract Territory. The remaining members of the new Social Committee are not sheikhs.

According to the Chief Sheikhs of the tribes living in the territory of the Upper Banop, these people cannot make any decisions and defend their interests on behalf of the entire population of the region. There is a risk that the policy of such a composition of the Committee will lead to an imbalance in inter-tribal relations and destabilize the situation in the Contract area. The mayors of Dokemy district and Third Village district share this opinion. The second composition of the Social Committee needed to be revised.

Eventually, all parties agreed that the Social Committee should include representatives of the local authorities of the Sadbokan Governorate, the Sadbokan Provincial Council, and the Atukaz State Oil Company. Creating and using such organizational units as the Social Committee in the name of the company's interests is just one example of demonstrating the elements of an innovative model for assessing stakeholders and implementing the Stakeholder Engagement Plan. This forward-thinking approach not only ensures the project's success but also paves the way for future sustainable development initiatives.

HOW TO CHOOSE CSR METHODOLOGY

Correctly chosen CRS methodology plays a decisive role in securing and developing the projects. Previously, many companies, including oil companies, relied on surveys to devise their CSR programs. Some companies still do. Most surveys and studies concerning the field of CSR have been conducted with the consumer in mind. For example, researchers have established that a company's CSR programs have to satisfy customers, and they will move toward products and companies. There are many other polls, but they all concentrate on what consumers think about a company's product or services, depending on its CSR programs.

The 3D CSR methodology, which stands for data-driven, diverse, and decentralized CSR, involves developing unique methods for collecting important information to create the company's CSR programs instead of relying on surveys, which focus on the level of consumer loyalty to the company's product.

The 3D CSR methodology stands out for its unique approach.

First, it gathers a substantial amount of data related to socio-demographic characteristics such as median age, educational attainment, crime rates, unemployment rates, family composition, tribal relations, employability of the workforce, as well as various relevant political, economic, religious, cultural, and social factors to assess the needs of each local community in the areas of education, training, employment, health, economic development, and infrastructure. For instance, in a mining project, the methodology would consider the impact on local water sources, air quality, and biodiversity. This innovative data-driven approach sets it apart from traditional CSR methods.

Second, it develops a set of processes, mechanisms, and incentives to engage and compensate the various stakeholders in each community as well as resolve conflicts. For example, it creates conditions through social responsibility committees for local tribal leaders and officials to be involved in resolving problems based on mutual interests. The Social Responsibility Committees are composed of representatives of local tribes, the State Company, and members of the Local Council. This methodology also develops a grievance mechanism for handling complaints from the local communities, including all population segments. It creates a fair employment system for thousands of former land users and their families. These mechanisms ensure that the interests of all stakeholders are considered and addressed, promoting a harmonious relationship between the company and the community.

The 3D CSR methodology offers a more comprehensive and practical approach than traditional CSR frameworks that rely on polls and surveys. Its analytical depth, encompassing a wide range of variables to assess community needs, has a proven track record of success. This not only makes it a compelling choice for multinational companies seeking to enhance their CSR strategies but also instills a sense of hope and optimism for a more inclusive and sustainable future.

Undoubtedly, the role of the 3D CSR methodology is even more crucial for the success of multinational companies operating across diverse sectors. Its unique approach to data collection, stakeholder engagement, and conflict resolution can significantly enhance the effectiveness of CSR strategies in these complex business environments.

For a business firm that functions to produce profits, this 3D CSR model is becoming more and more in demand. It becomes truly indispensable during the transition of wild capitalism style business to a social system. The purpose of a business is still the production of wealth. However, it does this as a social organization forced to respond to the demands of society and its citizens. That is why a 3D CSR model will have a substantial positive impact and help fully integrate the interests and needs of communities, business operations, and shareholders into CSR strategies. This approach can generate more profit and growth in the long run, as my track record, which includes successful implementations of the 3D CSR methodology in various continents, has amply demonstrated.

The CSR function has evolved into a crucial factor in shaping a company's competitiveness and reputation. This is particularly true for firms in sectors with close ties to their social environment, such as international corporations managing projects in resource-rich emerging countries. The 3D CSR

220

methodology, with its innovative and integrated approach, is well suited to solving these problems.

The 3D methodology developed by the author in the CSR field is innovative, comprehensive, and duplicable. The essential elements of his methodology consist of the following:

1. Creating a mechanism for conflict resolution in the form of special resolution social committees (the "Social Committee") consisting of local government officials, indigenous population representatives, and company representatives;

2. Recommending to the company the nature and level of its social participation in CSR programs, such as training and employing the local population and financial involvement in the local business projects aimed at improving the necessary industrial infrastructure and trade;

3. The 3D CSR methodology is adaptable and can be modified and corrected as needed to reflect the political and economic realities of a particular region. However, it's important to note that this adaptability may also present challenges, as it requires a deep understanding of the local context and the ability to adjust strategies accordingly. Despite these potential challenges, the adaptability of the methodology is a key strength, reassuring multinational companies that they can successfully handle the unique challenges and opportunities of operating in resource-rich emerging countries.

4. Negotiating business deals with the local government, including the indigenous population's interests.

Another unorthodox element of the 3D CSR method lies in the fact that this method rejects a traditional "win-win" business formula for success, having added a third party to the equation: the local people. For the first time, the business formula utilized by a multinational corporation began to look like a "win-win-win" situation, heeding the fact that the benefit to the government does not necessarily translate into the benefit for the indigenous population.

Behind the simplicity of this formula, there are complex mathematical calculations based on relevant risk assessments. These calculations are based on advanced statistical models and econometric techniques, ensuring the robustness and reliability of the methodology. Political and economic scenarios and reasonable assumptions in the 3D CSR stakeholder engagement plan involve the costs of civil strife, blockages, increased security, and other costs associated with tensions with local people who have the right to participate in developing their country.

Unfortunately, I will not disclose all aspects of my innovative 3D CSR methodology for interacting with stakeholders in the book. Rest assured, these aspects and tools are successfully applied when I work with the clients of my Consulting company.

The core of my method is its dynamic nature, which enables the transformation of initially flat and linear tables and data into a three-dimensional figure. Numerous ever-changing internal connections characterize this figure. These connections, which form, dissolve, and reemerge, provide a unique perspective on the seemingly linear stakeholder relationships.

The relationships that project stakeholders have with each other in the initial stage without the company's involvement and in the second stage, after the company's emergence and project development, serve as the basis for a unique 3D stakeholder engagement plan along the line Company—Stakeholder.

REFERENCES

International Finance Corporation. 2012. Performance Standards on Environmental and Social Sustainability

https://www.ifc.org/content/dam/ifc/doc/2010/2012-ifc-performance-standards-en.pdf

International Finance Corporation. 2006. Performance Standard 5 - Land Acquisition and Involuntary Resettlement

https://www.ifc.org/content/dam/ifc/doc/2000/2006-ifc-performance-standard-5-en.pdf

International Finance Corporation. 2012. Performance Standard 1 - Assessment and Management of Environmental and Social Risks and Impacts

https://www.ifc.org/content/dam/ifc/doc/2010/2012-ifc-performance-standard-1-en.pdf

International Finance Corporation. 2012. Performance Standard 5 - Land Acquisition and Involuntary Resettlement

https://www.ifc.org/content/dam/ifc/doc/2010/2012-ifc-performance-standard-5-en.pdf

International Finance Corporation. 2012. Performance Standard 7 - Indigenous Peoples

https://www.ifc.org/content/dam/ifc/doc/2010/2012-ifc-performance-standard-7-en.pdf

International Finance Corporation. 2002. Handbook for preparing a Resettlement Action Plan.

Guidelines prepared by IFC, Washington DC, USA

https://documents1.worldbank.org/curated/en/49279146815
3884773/pdf/246740PUB0REPL020020Box12600PUBLIC0.p
df

World Bank Group Corporate Social Responsibility Practice,
2004. Company Codes of Conduct and

International Standards: An Analytical Comparison, Part II of
II, Oil, Gas and Mining

https://documents1.worldbank.org/curated/en/44269146834
9802764/pdf/346620v20CompanyCodesofConduct.pdf

World Bank. 2001. The World Bank Operational Manual
4.12 - Involuntary Resettlement

https://thedocs.worldbank.org/en/doc/171c4239aa97b62d02
eb298f955a9f0a-0290012023/original/BP-4-12-Involuntary-
Resettlement.pdf